Hors d'Oeuvre at Home

with The Culinary Institute of America

Hors d'Oeuvre at Home

with The Culinary Institute of America

BICENTENNIAL
1807
WILEY
2007
BICENTENNIAL

JOHN WILEY & SONS, INC.

THE CULINARY INSTITUTE OF AMERICA

President: Dr. Tim Ryan

Vice-President, Continuing Education: Mark Erickson

Director of Intellectual Property: Nathalie Fischer

Managing Editor: Kate McBride

Editorial Project Manager: Lisa Lahey

Editorial Assistant: Margaret Wheeler

Production Assistant: Patrick Decker

Special thanks to Chef Gerard Viverito for his support and recipe contribution.

Published by John Wiley & Sons, Inc., Hoboken, New Jersey
Published simultaneously in Canada

For general information about our other products and services, please contact our Customer Care Department within the United States at (800) 762-2974, outside the United States at (317) 572-3993 or fax (317) 572-4002.

Wiley also publishes its books in a variety of electronic formats. Some content that appears in print may not be available in electronic books. For more information about Wiley products, visit our web site at www.wiley.com.

LIBRARY OF CONGRESS CATALOGING-IN-PUBLICATION DATA

Hors d'oeuvre at home with the Culinary Institute of America.
    p. cm.
  Includes index.
  ISBN 978-0-7645-9562-2 (cloth)
  1. Appetizers. I. Culinary Institute of America.
  TX740.H64474 2007
  641.8'12--dc22

Book designed and composed by Kevin Hanek
Set in Adobe Minion

Photography © Ben Fink
Photo on page i: Raspberry Rugalach (page 201); photo on page ii: Lamb Brochettes with Mint Pesto (page 111); photo on opposite page: Roasted Pepper and Eggplant Terrine (page 152); photo on pages vi–vii: Marinated Bocconcini (page 169)

Wiley bicentennial logo designed by Richard J. Pacifico

Printed in China
This book is printed on acid-free paper. ∞

10 9 8 7 6 5 4 3

Contents

Chapter One

INTRODUCTION

❦

T HE FRENCH TERM, *hors d'oeuvre,* translated literally means "outside the meal." Although hors d'oeuvre are typically served casually with drinks before a meal, they are an integral part of the dining experience. At parties and social gatherings, often hors d'oeuvre replace a traditional multicourse menu, and with great success; guests can stand and talk while they enjoy a dazzling range of choices of small bites.

The appeal of hors d'oeuvre is multifaceted. They stimulate the eyes and taste buds and tease the appetite. Cooks of all skill levels can confidently compile a reliable hors d'oeuvre repertoire that is simple to prepare, present, and clean up.

The hors d'oeuvre tradition can be found in most cuisines around the world. In Russia, the *zakushi* table served before banquets features bite-size treats, such as smoked and pickled fish, blinis with caviar, and special salads. In Scandinavia, a smorgasbord presents specialty dishes, including herring, cheeses, and pickled foods. Spanish cuisine offers bite-size tapas, which means "covers." The name *tapa* comes from the piece of bread that was once frequently used in bars to cover a glass of sherry and keep fruit flies from landing in the sherry. Barkeeps competed to top the bread with tantalizing foods, and when plates replaced the bread, an entirely new way of presenting and serving food began.

Throughout the Mediterranean regions, "little dishes" are known as *mezzes,* antipasti, or *chicchetti.* These small before-dinner dishes typically contain various types of olives, nuts, dips, spreads, and heavily seasoned items, such as grilled meat or fish kebabs.

In America, hors d'oeuvre incorporate all of the world's traditions, resulting in new and exciting ways to prepare and serve international favorites.

BASIC COMPONENTS AND PRINCIPLES

Preparation of some hors d'oeuvre requires nothing more than slicing the components and arranging the presentation, but some require more effort. Following are some examples of low-maintenance hors d'oeuvre:

- *Nuts, plain or marinated olives, and hard-boiled eggs.*

- *Dips and spreads accompanied by crudités (raw or chilled lightly blanched vegetables), crackers, or chips.*

- *Sausages, pâtés, terrines, thinly sliced or hand-carved smoked fish and meats, and cheeses served as reception or buffet items.*

- *Freshly shucked clams with Salsa Verde (page 43).*

- *Caviar, featured on its own, in special iced containers with mother of pearl or glass spoons so as not to affect the delicate flavor. Accompany with toast points, brioche, or blinis—perhaps with a dollop of crème fraîche.*

Other hors d'oeuvre will require more preparation. Composed hors d'oeuvre are constructed from two or more components, and while many components can be prepared in advance, often the final assembly and garnish has to be done at essentially the last moment, often to keep the filling from soaking into a crisp container or base, such as small rounds of toast, cream puffs or éclairs, and various kinds and shapes of pastry. These special items—including crostini and canapés, profiteroles, and tartlets and barquettes—add greatly to the variety and sophistication of the menu. Cured and smoked foods, pâtés, foie gras, salads, and vegetables are all appropriate as elements in any composed hors d'oeuvre. One special item, savory mousse, can be featured as a spread, piped into molds or edible containers, rolled into a roulade

and sliced, or shaped into quenelles (light poached dumplings traditionally oval in shape).

In selecting a suitable hors d'oeuvre menu, follow these basic rules:

1. *The nature of the event, along with the menu that follows the hors d'oeuvre, will dictate the amount of food to be prepared as hors d'oeuvre.*

2. *Think of visual appeal. Uncooked rice, beans, or small grains help to keep individual pieces from moving around on a platter and also add touches of texture and contrast to your buffet table. Use dramatic ice beds to keep seafood and caviar cold, but have a plan to contain the water from the ice as it melts.*

3. *Even the presentation of butler-style hors d'oeuvre or those served on platters requires forethought; for example, the person taking the last hors d'oeuvre should not have to sift through discarded garnishes.*

4. *Using handcrafted plates and containers can result in a unique presentation. However, an uneven surface, such as that often found on a handmade item, does require attention. Arrange items in such a way that they do not roll out of place on the uneven surface.*

HOW TO SELECT THE HORS D'OEUVRE FOR YOUR MENU AND HOW MUCH TO SERVE

When determining what hors d'oeuvre to offer, there are important factors to consider. For example, the season, the guests who will be dining, and, of course, the amount of money to be spent for the food items that will comprise the hors d'oeuvre. The price range determines, to some extent, the number of options that can be offered, and pricing will have an impact on the specific ingredients chosen. The number of guests will affect how much of each hors d'oeuvre to serve. In terms of portion, hors d'oeuvre should be readily ingested in one bite, with minimal mess and

Lemon Meringue Tatlets (page 185)

clean up. On some occasions, guests will expect certain food items to be served. For example, a daytime summer party or event may call for the inclusion of fruits and vegetables in the hors d'oeuvre offering. The food served at any event or celebration enhances the occasion. If a theme is maintained throughout the hors d'oeuvre presentation, guests will recognize it.

SELECTING BEVERAGES THAT COMPLEMENT THE FOOD

Of equal importance to the selection of the hors d'oeuvre are the accompanying beverages. The drink menu complements the food items in taste, texture, and color.

PRESENTATION: PASSED VERSUS STATIONARY

In every food offering, particularly in the case of hors d'oeuvre, the presentation of the items is important in creating their allure to guests. Any cuts or edges should be straight and neat; clear and precise angles will also enhance the attractiveness of hors d'oeuvre. For many events, hors d'oeuvre are served on platters or a trays. Guests will select the hors d'oeuvre based on their eye-appeal and possibly aromas. Neatness on the trays will contribute to the overall impact of the presentation. This is also true for hors d'oeuvre offered on banquet tables. For foods served on a platter, observe the spacing between pieces, as no guest will want to take hors d'oeuvre that have been touched by others.

For stationary hors d'oeuvre offerings, a buffet table is often required and some practical considerations need to be kept in mind. Provide adequate space for guests to move around and between any stationary hors d'oeuvre offerings. The food should be accessible not only to guests but also to attendants to replenish the dishes. Close placement to the kitchen will ensure that food is delivered quickly, so that it tastes and looks fresher.

Balance of a buffet is achieved by combining the physical aspects of food in the context of specific design principles. The food itself supplies the important visual elements: color, texture, and shape. It should also supply two important, but non-visual, elements: aroma and flavor. The design principles available for making these elements into beautiful arrangements include symmetrical or asymmetrical compositions, contrasting or complementary arrangements, and the use of lines to create patterns or indicate motion.

A food's natural color is one important tool in platter presentation and can be used as an element in design. We associate with colors in very specific ways: greens give the impression of freshness and vitality; browns, golds, and maroons are warming, comforting, and rich; and orange and red are intense, powerful colors. Colors that harmonize are those that touch each other on the color wheel (for example, green, blue, and violet are complementary colors, whereas blue and orange are contrasting). Clashing colors are rarely a problem as the natural colors of food generally harmonize well regardless of the item and its orientation to another of a different type. A greater concern is the overuse of one color in a single display.

Texture is important not only to the way the food looks, but also how it feels in our mouths. The surface of a food will either reflect or absorb light, making some foods glossy and others matte. Some foods have highly textured exteriors, whereas others are smooth. How food feels when it is bitten into is another aspect of texture that needs to be considered, as too much of the same texture is monotonous.

When creating a balanced presentation consider the accessibility of each item placed on the platter. Position taller items in the rear and shorter items in front. Place frequently accessed dispensers, such as sauceboats, in an area that does not disturb the design but allows guests easy access. A certain amount of regularity and repetition is comfortable and appealing, but too much of anything becomes monotonous, whether it is an ingredient, a color, a shape, a flavor, or a texture. Introducing contrasting elements adds energy and motion to an arrangement, but cohesion is essential; when every element seems to stand on its own, the effect can be chaotic.

The shape and height of the food is an important part of buffet presentation. Food has three dimensions: cubes, cylinders, spheres, and pyramids are just some of the shapes that food can assume. Alternating or repeating shapes in a design is one way to add visual interest to food arrangements. The natural shape of a food can be altered by cutting or slicing it. To give height to foods, roll or fold them, arrange them in piles or pyramids, or use serving pieces, such as pedestals, columns, or baskets, to raise them.

A focal point, the place at which the eyes converge, serves an important function on a platter. It introduces a large shape in a field of smaller shapes, it adds height. It can make the arrangement logical and sensible to the guest; one common focal point is simply a large or instantly identifiable item, such as a roast leg of lamb or a terrine, left intact and arranged on the platter. Sometimes, one or more garnish elements serve as the common focal point.

In order to have strong, clean lines arrange the food neatly and logically. Lines can be straight, curved, or angled. When a line is repeated, a pattern is created. The more evenly the lines are spaced, the more obvious is the pattern. The wider the spaces, the more obvious they are as discrete lines. When two lines meet, they create a shape, and within it is the focal point. Lines can move away from or toward this point and, thereby, introduce a sense of flow or motion into the arrangement.

The layout of the platter can be symmetrical or asymmetrical. The position of the focal point on a platter or plate determines how the food is arranged. A focal point positioned off center indicates that one side of the arrangement appears to have more weight than the other; positioning the focal point in the center gives the impression that both sides of the arrangement are in equilibrium. Asymmetrical arrangements tend to look natural, whereas symmetrical arrangements look formal.

PLANNING FOR WASTE

Ideally, hors d'oeuvre should result in little waste. However, some foods naturally generate waste, such as shrimp shells, skewers, or strawberry stems, and it will be necessary to consider any potential waste. For passed hors d'oeuvre, guests will generally lay any waste on trays as they go by.

It is a good idea to place a few trays strategically with planted waste already on them (such as one or two stems or a used skewer) so that guests know where to leave waste. For stationary hors d'oeuvre presentations, clear away waste periodically so as not to detract from the overall food presentation.

MAKING APPETIZERS FROM HORS D'OEUVRE

To create appetizers from hors d'oeuvre, the portion size can be increased. However, the appetizer sizes should be sensible, and be smaller than what would be offered on an à la carte meal menu. Guests will want to sample a few appetizers without filling up, so that they can still enjoy the main course and dessert.

PLATING AND PRESENTING APPETIZERS

The following basic principles will be helpful as you select, plate, and prepare appetizers and hors d'oeuvre:

1. *Serve appetizers at the correct temperature; you may need to warm or chill plates.*

2. *Appetizers' purpose is to stimulate guests' appetites. For this reason, proper and meticulous seasoning is extremely important.*

3. *The shaping and portion of an appetizer is crucial. Offer just enough to make the appetizer appealing, but not so much that the guest will feel overwhelmed by the portion.*

4. *The appetizer will create a first impression on the guest. Guests may judge the entire meal just by the neatness of the appetizer.*

5. *For shared appetizers, consider splitting the portion prior to it being served to the guest.*

6. *The correct size and shape for serving pieces will add to an appetizer's overall effect. Color, shape, and leftover space all play a role in the appeal of an appetizer. Provide guests will all items necessary to the appetizer, such as cups for dipping sauces.*

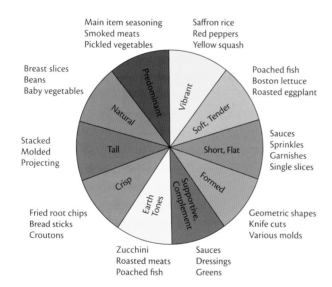

ABOVE: *Plated appetizer composition balance wheel*
AT RIGHT: *Roated Pepper Salad (page 135)*

Chapter Two

HORS D'OEUVRE IN BITE-SIZE CONTAINERS

ONE OF THE most enticing characteristics of hors d'oeuvre is that they are primarily finger foods, with all of their components edible. The first step in creating many hors d'oeuvre is to choose the container or base—typically made from bread, dough, vegetables, or fruits—that will aesthetically and flavorfully complement the filling or toppings.

BREADS

Almost any type of bread can be used to hold an hors d'oeuvre topping or dip—white, whole wheat, rye, multigrain. The thickness of the bread when sliced should be uniform, but must be relatively thin. If the bread is not firm enough to hold the topping, toast it. It should neither be too crisp or too soft—not hard enough to shatter when bitten, but stiff enough to hold the selection of toppings without collapsing.

Cut sliced breads into a variety of shapes to add interest or eye appeal to any hors d'oeuvre display. First, remove the crusts from a short stack of slices and then cut the stack diagonally each way to form into triangles or crosswise each way to create squares. To cut other shapes, such as rounds, crescents, or hexagons, use cookie cutters to maintain uniformity. Many small items of uniform size and shape look very impressive when served on a tray or platter—inconsistency always tends to look messy.

Crisp flatbreads or crackers do not require toasting and are often a good choice to use as a base for hors d'oeuvre, but should be bite-size. They are crisper than bread and may tend to break apart when bitten, making eating difficult if they are two bites in size rather than one.

BREAD STICKS

Add a festive touch to almost any hors d'oeuvre buffet with an assortment of bread sticks. Serve them in bunches, displayed in baskets or standing in cups, to add some dramatic height to your food display.

Bread sticks are easily made from almost any yeast-raised bread dough. Allow the dough to relax before rolling so it can be stretched until it is fairly thin. Cut the dough into narrow strips that will bake to crisp sticks.

For added color and flavor, knead herbs and enrichments, such as grated hard cheeses or minced olives or sun dried tomatoes into the dough before it is stretched or rolled out and cut. Another simple but flavorful touch is to lightly brush the bread sticks with extra-virgin olive oil and sprinkle with some kosher or sea salt just as they come piping hot from the oven.

DOUGHS

Several types of dough, such as pâte à choux, puff pastry, and phyllo, make excellent containers and bases for hors d'oeuvre. Whatever dough is used in the hors d'oeuvre can be made well before the filling, but the filling should not be placed in or on the container or base until just before serving time to prevent soggy hors d'oeuvre. The following pages contain a description of some of the most useful types of hors d'oeuvre doughs.

PÂTE À CHOUX Pâte à choux can be used in sweet or savory hors d'oeuvre recipes. Pâte à choux is a cooked batter that expands into a delicately crisp, hollow shell, and is remarkably versatile, for it can be used in savory hors d'oeuvre or sweet dessert recipes. The batter can be piped from a pastry bag into different shapes, to create cream puffs, profiteroles, and éclairs.

The batter includes water or milk, butter, flour, and eggs. A batter containing milk bakes differently than one with water because milk causes the pastry to bake and brown before the batter has dried out enough to become crisp, but the milk solids produce a more tender and flavorful pastry than one made with water. When water or milk is used in a choux batter, set the oven at a very high temperature so the batter will expand fully and quickly, and then lower the temperature to dry out the pastry. This will result in a fully dried, crisp, and light pastry.

LAMINATED DOUGH There are different types of dough that can be called "laminated" and are among the more difficult doughs to create. The laminated dough category includes the similar, yet distinct, doughs used in Danishes, croissants, and puff pastries. Laminated dough is often used in preparing barquettes, tartlets, cheese sticks, and sweet or savory palmiers (also known as palm leaves or elephant ears).

To produce laminated dough that is flaky and delicate, use proper mixing methods, rolling techniques, and careful temperature control during baking. Begin with basic dough. For croissant, lean yeast dough is best. For Danish, yeast dough enriched with milk and eggs is the starting point. For puff pastry (pâte feuilletée) and blitz puff pastry, use dough without added leavening. If yeast is included in the dough, allow time for the dough to relax and the yeast to ferment.

All types of laminated dough are layered with butter or butter with shortening, which has a leavening effect and produces a flaky consistency after baking; flour can also be added to the roll-in. The rolled-in butter creates the distinct layers that contribute to these unique dough types. Use chilled but not extremely hard butter for the roll-in. After

blending, transfer the dough to sheet pans lined with parchment and chill the dough until it is firm but not brittle.

Once the dough has chilled, use a pastry brush to remove excess flour from the surface of the dough. Roll the dough into sheets and cut it into the desired shapes using cutters or sharp knives.

When working with dough, observe the following guidelines:

1. *Take out only the amount of dough you will be working with at a given time; keep the rest of the dough chilled. (Dough that is allowed to rest at room temperature before rolling, cutting, and shaping will result in decreased flakiness of the finished product.)*

2. *Clean cuts will ensure even rising, so use a sharp knife or cutter for cutting or shaping the dough (especially with high, straight-sided pastry containers such as vol-au-vent and bouchée).*

3. *Roll the dough up to the edges but not over them or you will destroy the layers at the edges and the dough will rise unevenly.*

4. *For puff pastry, it is important to refrigerate the dough before baking. The chilling will keep the dough layers and butter or butter and shortening roll-in separate, and produce the best rise and flakiness.*

5. *Save scraps from puff pastry. Combine them and roll out to make pastries that do not require substantial rise, such as napoleons.*

PHYLLO DOUGH Phyllo dough is often used to prepare strudel and baklava. The dough is low in fat as it is made only of flour, water, and, in some cases, a small amount of oil. Many professional chefs actually prefer to purchase phyllo dough premade and frozen. It takes some time for frozen phyllo dough to come to room temperature. To ensure the dough doesn't dry out as you are working, remove it from the wrapping and keep it covered with dampened towels or a sheet of plastic wrap.

Spread, spray, or brush the dough sheets evenly with melted butter, or with equal amounts of butter and bread crumbs, as you layer the dough, to keep the phyllo layers separate as the dough bakes for a flakiness that is similar to a puff pastry.

To help the layers remain separate and rise more during baking, refrigerate the phyllo pastries until ready to bake.

CRACKERS

Crackers are a perfect crispy accompaniment to an hors d'oeuvre spread, and there are different ways to produce them. For icebox crackers, prepare a savory dough, shape it into a log, and chill until firm. Slice the log crosswise into thin rounds and bake until crisp. Some crackers are made from baked batter that can be shaped when warm by pressing them into cups or other molds or draping them over rolling pins. If seasoning crackers with nuts and seeds, consider flavors that will complement the various foods in the hors d'oeuvre spread.

CRISPS

Potato crisps, or chips, are made by thinly slicing potatoes and frying the slices in oil until crisp. Some less obvious choices for a crisp base are vegetables and fruits such as sweet potatoes, beets, artichokes, pears, apples, and bananas.

VEGETABLES AND FRUIT

Vegetables and fruit make colorful, convenient, and easy-to-prepare containers and bases for hors d'oeuvre. Preparation time tends to be significantly shorter than for many other edible containers; in some cases, the chef simply needs to wash, peel, remove seeds, or hollow out the vegetable or fruit. As with other containers and bases for hors d'oeuvre, serve flavors that complement the fillings and toppings on the hors d'oeuvre menu. These natural containers include:

1. *Vegetables with a natural curve to contain smooth mixtures, such as mousses, tapenades, or spreads, that can be spooned or piped in:*

   - *Belgian endive, celery, mushroom caps.*

2. *Vegetables that can be hollowed out to create a bite-size cup and filled with a filling or dip:*

   - *Cucumbers, radishes, cherry tomatoes, grapes.*

ALMOST HOMEMADE

Frozen Dough

Most supermarkets offer different types of high-quality frozen dough that is perfect for making containers and bases for hors d'oeuvre. The great advantage to buying a premade dough is that more time and effort can go into creating fillings and toppings for it—they are what will make the greatest visual impact. Always conduct a taste test before using any type of premade product, especially one that will be served to guests.

Phyllo dough is commonly available frozen in markets. This versatile pastry dough is commonly layered or rolled up with filling, but may be made into small cups or containers to be used for any of a variety of fillings.

Use 4-fl oz or 2-fl oz miniature muffin tins. Cut the sheets of phyllo pastry into 3-in squares. Brush the squares lightly on one side with melted butter and layer them 3 to 4 in a stack. Brush the inside of the muffin tins lightly with melted butter and press a stack of phyllo inside each of the wells in the muffin tin, pressing the pastry to the bottom and sides. Bake in a preheated 350°F oven until the pastry is golden brown, about 15 minutes.

Puff pastry dough is also available frozen in many markets. It is available in sheets or often in convenient, ready-to-bake, vol-au-vent containers. A vol-au-vent is a puff pastry shell cut and shaped so that as it bakes, the sides rise or puff and the center remains depressed, creating a small edible container that may be filled with a savory mousse (e.g., Smoked Salmon Mousse, page 62) or fresh berries and a sprig of mint. Vols-au-vent instantly add a flair of sophistication to any hors d'oeuvre table.

Pâte à Choux and Gougères

MAKES ABOUT 68 BITE-SIZE GOUGÈRES

THESE TASTY treats look beautiful served in a linen-lined basket, but for a more formal event, cut them in half, fill with Smoked Salmon Mousse (page 62) or Foie Gras Mousse (page 63), and arrange them on a platter.

1 cup milk

½ cup (1 stick) butter

½ tsp sugar

½ tsp salt

1 cup bread flour

4 large eggs

pinch of cayenne

½ cup grated Gruyère cheese

1. Bring the milk, butter, sugar, and salt to a boil over medium heat, stirring constantly. Remove from the heat, add the flour all at once, and stir vigorously to combine. Return the pan to medium heat and cook, stirring constantly, until the mixture pulls away from the sides of the pan, about 2 minutes.

2. Transfer the mixture to the bowl of a stand mixer and beat briefly on medium speed with a paddle attachment. Add the eggs two at a time, beating until smooth after each addition. Add the cayenne and cheese and mix until blended.

3. Fill a pastry bag fitted with a medium plain tip and pipe ¾-in domes of batter onto parchment-lined sheet pans.

4. Bake in a preheated 350°F oven until the pastries are puffed and golden brown, about 35 minutes.

NOTE: For a drier and deeper blond pâte à choux, substitute an equal part of water for the milk. For a shiny finish, brush the pâte à choux with egg wash (1 egg whisked with 2 Tbsp water) prior to baking.

To make plain pâte à choux, omit the cayenne and Gruyère cheese.

VARIATIONS

HERB TOMATO GOUGÈRES: Substitute ⅓ cup olive oil for the butter in the above recipe. Omit the cayenne and Gruyère. Add the following garnish to the finished pâte à choux in Step 2: a pinch ground black pepper, 1 Tbsp finely chopped oil-packed sun-dried tomatoes, 1 Tbsp finely chopped basil, and 1¼ tsp finely chopped thyme. Pipe and bake as directed.

CHOCOLATE PÂTE À CHOUX: Substitute sifted cocoa powder for 1 Tbsp of the flour. Increase the amount of sugar by 2¼ tsp and omit the cayenne and Gruyère in the above recipe. Mix, pipe, and bake as directed.

AT LEFT: Pâte à choux is a crisp and delicious support for both sweet and savory flavors. The eggy pastry dough can be piped into many different shapes and sizes.

Blitz Puff Pastry

*M*AKING PUFF pastry is a difficult and time consuming undertaking. This "Blitz" recipe allows even the busiest of cooks to make this delicious pastry fresh. Use it for making Cheese Sticks (Paillettes; recipe follows) and small containers or bases to hold any filling or topping of your choice.

2 cups bread flour

2 cups pastry flour

2 cups (4 sticks) cold butter, cut into ½-in cubes

2 tsp salt

1 cup ice water

1. Sift the flours into a bowl or onto a table surface. Drop in the cubes of butter and coat with flour. Make a well in the flour mixture.

2. Dissolve the salt in the water and pour into the well.

3. Combine all ingredients to form a loose, shaggy mass.

4. On a floured surface, roll the dough into a ½-in-thick rectangle. With the rectangle arranged horizontally on the work surface, fold both the right and left sides into the center, so they meet like an open book and create a neat seam. Fold up the sides as if closing a book. Turn the pastry so the "spine" side is to the left.

5. Roll out the dough to a ½-in-thick rectangle and repeat Step 4 two or three times, allowing the dough to rest 30 minutes in between each fold. Roll out the dough again before use as recipe directs.

STORAGE: Wrap the dough tightly in plastic wrap and store in the refrigerator for up to 3 days.

NOTE: More folds will yield finer and more even layers with less height. Fewer folds yield a lighter product, with irregular layers and more height.

CHEESE STICKS (PAILLETTES)

MAKES 30 CHEESE STICKS

BE CREATIVE with Cheese Sticks—substitute different cheeses and spices to create different flavors to fit the theme of any occasion. You can also twist the strips of dough like a corkscrew before baking as a design element or to denote different flavors.

1 large egg yolk

1 Tbsp whole milk

1 lb Blitz Puff Pastry

¼ cup grated Parmesan cheese

sweet Spanish paprika for sprinkling on pastry

1. Whisk together the egg yolk and milk in a cup to make an egg wash. Brush the puff pastry sheet with the egg wash.

2. Sprinkle the cheese and paprika evenly over the puff pastry sheet. Cut the sheet lengthwise into ¼-in strips.

3. Bake the cheese sticks on parchment-lined sheet pans in a preheated 400°F oven until golden brown, about 10 minutes.

NOTE: Cayenne, poppy seeds, or sesame seeds may be used as alternative garnishes to the paprika.

Folding Blitz Puff Pastry creates layers within the dough that trap moisture and add volume to the finished baked product.

Palmiers with Prosciutto

MAKES 40 TO 45 PALMIERS

THIS PASTRY gets its name from the shape it forms as the result of folding and baking. Make these in batches ahead of time and store them unbaked in logs tightly wrapped in plastic wrap in the freezer. Slice and bake them as needed; slicing them frozen is easy when using a serrated knife.

8 oz Blitz Puff Pastry (page 16)

¼ cup tomato paste

12 thin slices prosciutto

½ cup finely grated Parmesan cheese

1. Roll out the puff pastry on the work surface to a 10 × 10-in square and brush with a small amount of the tomato paste.

2. Lay prosciutto over the puff pastry and dust with the cheese. Roll each long side in toward center until they meet. Fold one long side over the other. Slice the pastry crosswise into pieces ¼ in thick and place cut side down on parchment-lined sheet pans. Bake in a preheated 400°F oven until golden brown, about 10 minutes.

NOTE: Place another piece of parchment paper on top of the pastries as they bake to help the pieces stay flat. Remove the top piece for the last few minutes to allow the palmier tops to brown.

AT RIGHT: When making palmiers, the dough must be uniformly rolled out with equal folding to ensure that the product bakes evenly.

Grissini

*M*AKE EXTRA of these hard-to-resist bread sticks. Serve them in baskets, or standing tall in a beautiful glass or ceramic jar with a variety of dips. Serve any leftover grissini with a hearty soup or a beautiful green salad.

cornmeal for dusting

2¼ cups water

1 Tbsp compressed yeast

4 Tbsp extra-virgin olive oil plus extra for brushing the grissini

6¾ cups bread flour

2 tsp salt

egg wash (1 large egg beaten with 2 Tbsp water)

GARNISH OPTIONS

sea salt for sprinkling

sesame seeds for sprinkling

chopped herbs such as basil and oregano

1. Line sheet pans with parchment or dust with cornmeal.

2. Combine the water, yeast, and oil until yeast is dissolved. Add the flour and salt. Mix the dough until smooth and elastic. Cover the bowl with plastic wrap and allow the dough to ferment until double in bulk, about 1 hour 15 minutes.

3. Fold over the dough, break it into 1½-oz pieces, and shape each piece into a ball. Place the balls on a parchment-lined sheet pan and let proof for 1 hour.

4. Roll the balls into long, thin sticks. Place the sticks on the baking sheets, brush with olive oil or egg wash, and top with desired seasoning. Pan-proof the grissini for 15 minutes.

5. Bake the grissini in a preheated 425°F oven until crisp, 10 to 12 minutes.

STORAGE: Store any lefrover grissini in an airtight container at room temperature.

Chicken Croustade

MAKES 30 FILLED CROUSTADES

*T*HE PROSCIUTTO adds a delectable element to the flavor of this hors d'oeuvre. However, make sure to buy good-quality prosciutto, such as the imported Italian prosciutto di Parma, or the filling will be unpalatably salty.

1 loaf soft white bread, sliced

1 Tbsp olive oil plus extra for greasing the muffin tins

¾ cup heavy cream

8 oz raw chicken breast meat, cut into small dice

4 oz prosciutto, cut into small dice

pinch of ground black pepper or more to taste

1 large egg yolk

2 Tbsp grated Parmesan cheese, plus as needed for topping

1 Tbsp chopped basil

1 Tbsp chopped flat-leaf parsley

1 tsp salt

1. With a rolling pin, roll out each bread slice until thin. Cut out bread with plain 1½-in-diameter round cutter and flatten again with a rolling pin. Oil 30 small muffin tins and place the bread rounds inside. Bake in a preheated 325°F oven until golden. Store the croustade shells covered in a dry area until ready to use.

2. Boil the cream in a small pan until reduced by half and reserve until needed.

3. Sauté the chicken in the oil until half done. Add the prosciutto and continue to cook until the prosciutto is thoroughly heated and chicken is thoroughly cooked.

4. Add the reserved cream and black pepper; bring to a simmer. Temper the egg yolk in a bowl by adding about one-third of the hot cream, whisking constantly. Strain the egg-yolk mixture into the chicken mixture, being careful not to boil.

5. Add the cheese, basil, and parsley and season with salt.

6. Put the croustade shells on a sheet pan and fill with the chicken mixture; sprinkle with a little additional grated cheese and brown lightly under a broiler or salamander. Serve warm.

Sun-Dried Tomato and Goat's Milk Cheese Tartlets

MAKES 2½ DOZEN 1¾-IN TARTLETS

*E*ASY TO make and impressive to behold, these tartlets will dress up any occasion. They make a flavorful accompaniment to almost any hors d'oeuvre table.

1 lb Blitz Puff Pastry (page 16)

¾ cup milk

¼ cup dry sherry

3 Tbsp chopped basil

1 Tbsp minced garlic

1 tsp ground white pepper

3 large eggs

1 Tbsp all-purpose flour

4 oz fresh goat's milk cheese, crumbled

½ cup sun-dried tomatoes, minced

2 Tbsp minced green onions

1. Roll the puff pastry dough to ⅛ in thickness. Prick the dough with a fork.

2. Cut 30 rounds from the puff pastry using a 2-in round cutter and press gently into 30 1¾-in tart molds by "sandwiching" between two molds. Place the molds on a sheet pan.

3. Cover the dough in the molds with a small piece of foil and fill with uncooked dried beans or pastry weights. Bake in a 425°F oven for 5 minutes. Allow the tartlets to cool completely. Remove the foil and beans or weights.

4. Combine the milk, sherry, basil, garlic, and pepper in a food processor. Add the eggs and flour and process until just blended.

5. Toss together the goat's milk cheese, tomatoes, and green onions in a bowl.

6. Put 2½ tsp of the goat's milk cheese mixture into each tartlet.

7. Fill each tartlet two-thirds full with the egg mixture.

8. Bake the filled tartlets in a preheated 350°F oven until set, about 15 minutes.

AT LEFT: Tartlets are easily made by sandwiching rounds of cutout dough between two molds and baking them. Leaving the molds on the dough during baking is another way to help preserve the tartlet shape until the dough is finished baking.

Lobster and Prosciutto Crostini

MAKES 30 CROSTINI

LOBSTER TAKES center stage on any menu. Highlight these dramatically beautiful crostini on an hors d'oeuvre display and have enough for everyone to have a taste. Assemble these close to serving because the prosciutto and lobster will not hold long at room temperature.

1 baguette

1 cup Garlic and Parsley Compound Butter (recipe follows)

olive oil, for frying

30 sage leaves

7½ oz goat's milk cheese

8 oz thinly sliced prosciutto

8 oz lobster meat, cooked and chilled

1. Cut the baguette diagonally into thirty ¼-in-thick slices. Brush each slice with softened compound butter and toast briefly on a sheet pan in a preheated 400°F oven until slightly browned on the edges, 10 to 12 minutes.

2. Heat 1 in of olive oil in a small sauté pan. Put the sage leaves into the oil and lightly fry them for 2 to 3 minutes. Remove the leaves and drain on paper towels. Set aside at room temperature until needed.

3. Spread 1 Tbsp of the goat's milk cheese on each of the toasted baguette slices. Arrange 1 slice of the prosciutto on top of the cheese and top with 1 Tbsp of the lobster meat. Garnish each with a fried sage leaf. Serve immediately.

GARLIC AND PARSLEY COMPOUND BUTTER

MAKES ABOUT 32 TBSP (ABOUT 2 CUPS)

SERVE THIS flavorful butter not only on Lobster and Prosciutto Crostini, but also on crusty slices from a loaf of Italian bread—perfect with a bowl of pasta a la marinara. Spread the butter on slices of a baguette and toast them in the oven to make homemade croutons for salad.

3 garlic cloves, coarsely chopped

1½ bunches flat-leaf parsley, leaves only

1 tsp salt

2 cups (4 sticks) unsalted butter, cold,
    cut into small dice

1. Put the garlic, parsley, and salt in a food processor fitted with a blade attachment and pulse until the ingredients are evenly minced and the mixture is well blended.

2. Place the butter in a mixer fitted with a paddle attachment. Add the garlic-parsley mixture and blend on medium speed until the butter is softened and the mixture is blended well and a light green color.

3. Press the compound butter into ramekins. Cover with plastic wrap and refrigerate or freeze until needed. Or, shape the butter into a log on a piece of plastic wrap. Roll it into a 1-in cylinder and secure the ends by twisting. Chill until firm, about 2 hours. Remove the plastic from the log and cut the butter crosswise into rounds for serving.

Goat's Milk Cheese and Sweet Onion Crostini

MAKES 30 CROSTINI

*T*HERE ARE many different kinds of bread available, and nearly every type has the ability to be transformed into the small toasted bread slices called crostini. They are easy to create and are the basic building blocks of canapés because their durability and sturdiness make them ideal bases for all kinds of toppings.

1 baguette

1 cup Garlic and Parsley Compound Butter, soft (page 24)

1 lb 4 oz small white onions

3 Tbsp chopped sun-dried tomatoes

olive oil, for sautéing

1 garlic clove, chopped

1½ Tbsp sugar

2 Tbsp red wine vinegar

1 tsp salt

½ tsp ground black pepper

7½ oz goat's milk cheese

1. Cut the baguette diagonally into thirty ¼-in-thick slices. Brush each slice with softened compound butter and toast briefly on a sheet pan in a preheated 400°F oven until crisp and lightly browned around the edges, 10 to 12 minutes.

2. Roast the onions in a shallow pan in a 350°F oven until tender, 1½ to 2 hours. Allow to cool, then peel, cut into medium-dice pieces, and reserve in a bowl.

3. To prepare the topping, sweat the sun-dried tomatoes in a little olive oil over medium heat until slightly tender, about 10 minutes. Add the garlic and onions and continue to cook over low heat until the ingredients are warm and the flavors have blended together, stirring the mixture gently with a wooden spoon to prevent breaking up the ingredients, 10 to 15 minutes.

4. Add the sugar and vinegar. Season the mixture with salt and pepper.

5. Spread 1 Tbsp of the goat's milk cheese on each baguette slice, top with 1 Tbsp onion and sun-dried tomato mixture, and serve.

NOTE: Instead of using goat's milk cheese, substitute another soft spreadable cheese. Some good choices would be Boursin, Gorgonzola, or even drained ricotta cheese.

Spanikopita

*F*OLD THE phyllo dough carefully when making the individual spanikopita packets—the neater they are the more impressive they look. Do not overfill the packets or they may split open while they are baking.

1 Tbsp butter

¼ cup minced shallots

1 Tbsp minced garlic

6 oz spinach, cleaned and stems removed

½ tsp grated nutmeg

1½ tsp chopped dill

½ cup crumbled feta cheese

¼ cup grated mozzarella cheese

½ tsp salt

pinch of ground black pepper

6 sheets phyllo dough

⅓ cup butter, melted

1. Melt the butter in a sauté pan over medium heat until it starts to bubble. Add the shallots and garlic and sweat until translucent.

2. Add the spinach, nutmeg, and dill and sauté gently until the spinach is wilted, 1 to 2 minutes. Transfer the spinach mixture to a stainless-steel bowl and cool to room temperature. Add the cheeses and season with salt and pepper. Cover the filling and refrigerate until needed.

3. Lay 1 sheet of phyllo dough on a cutting board. Brush lightly with melted butter. Place another sheet of phyllo dough directly onto the buttered sheet and brush it lightly with butter. Repeat for a third time.

4. Cut the phyllo dough lengthwise into 6 even strips. Spoon 2 Tbsp spinach filling onto the bottom right corner of each strip. Fold the bottom right corner of a strip diagonally to the left side of the strip to create a triangle of dough encasing the filling. Fold the bottom left point of the dough up along the left side of the dough to seal in the filling.

5. Fold the bottom left corner of the dough diagonally to the right side of the dough to form a triangle. Fold the bottom right point up along the right edge of the dough. Repeat until the end of the strip is reached and you have a triangle of layered phyllo dough with the filling wrapped inside. Repeat with each strip.

6. Put the phyllo triangles on a parchment-lined sheet pan and brush each with melted butter.

7. Bake in a preheated 400°F oven until golden brown, 15 to 20 minutes. Serve immediately.

AT LEFT: When making pie-size or hors d'oeuvre–size spanikopita, keep the phyllo dough moist with melted butter to prevent it from drying out and cracking while folding.

Corn Tortilla Cups with Black Beans and Guacamole

*I*F SHORT on time, omit the stock and, rather than soak and cook dry beans, substitute canned black beans. Rinse and drain them well and add them to the sauté pan with the remaining ingredients.

8 oz black turtle beans, soaked overnight

1 cup onions, minced

3 garlic cloves, minced

2 jalapeños, minced

2 Tbsp vegetable oil plus oil for deep frying

¼ cup tomato paste

2 tsp ground cumin

2 tsp dried thyme

2 tsp dried oregano

vegetable stock for cooking beans

2 tsp salt or to taste

pinch of cayenne or to taste

3-in-diameter corn-tortilla rounds

3 cups Guacamole (recipe follows)

1. Soak the beans 8 hours or overnight in a deep saucepan in enough water to cover. Drain in a colander. Sweat the onions, garlic, and jalapeños in the oil in a large saucepan. Add the tomato paste, cumin, thyme, and oregano and sauté briefly. Add beans and enough stock to cover by 1 in and cook until tender, 2 to 3 hours, adding more stock if needed. Season with salt and cayenne.

2. Cut out tortillas into 3-in rounds with a plain cutter. Place a tortilla in a small ladle and squeeze down lightly with a slightly smaller ladle. This will result in a small tortilla cup.

3. Deep fry in oil at 350°F until crisp; drain and season with salt. Serve the black bean mixture and guacamole in the tortilla cups.

GUACAMOLE

MAKES 3 CUPS

EVERYONE LOVES guacamole, so make plenty. Use it to create an assortment of hors d'oeuvre; spread it on bread to make tea sandwiches with guacamole and thinly sliced Jack cheese, or spoon it on top of miniature quesadillas.

2 avocados, peeled, pitted, and cut into medium dice

2 tomatoes, chopped

½ red onion, cut into small mince

2 jalapeños, finely minced

1 lime, juiced

1 garlic clove, minced

1 tsp salt

¼ tsp ground black pepper

Combine all the ingredients in a bowl, cover, and refrigerate until needed.

The size of the cups can easily be adjusted by cutting out larger or smaller rounds from the tortillas and frying them in comparably sized baskets.

Red Pepper Mousse in Endive

THE NATURALLY curved shape of the endive leaves makes them a perfect container for many different fillings and spreads, such as Blue Cheese Mousse (page 163) or Smoked Salmon Mousse (page 62).

¾ cup minced onions

1 garlic clove, finely minced

2 Tbsp vegetable oil

3 red peppers, cut into small dice

1 cup chicken stock

pinch of saffron threads, crushed

2 Tbsp tomato paste

pinch of salt or more to taste

pinch of ground white pepper or more to taste

1 Tbsp powdered gelatin

¼ cup white wine

¾ cup heavy cream, whipped

30 Belgian endive leaves

GARNISH

30 slivers red pepper

1. Sauté the onions and garlic in the oil in a medium sauté pan until golden. Add the diced peppers, stock, saffron, tomato paste, salt, and pepper. Simmer until all ingredients are tender and the liquid is reduced by half.

2. Sprinkle the gelatin over the wine in a small bowl and stir to break up any clumps. Let the gelatin soften in the wine for about 3 minutes.

3. Purée the red pepper mixture in a blender. Add the gelatin while the red pepper mixture is still hot and blend to combine all ingredients well. Taste and add more salt and pepper if needed. Pour into a bowl.

4. Cool the red pepper mixture over an ice bath until it mounds when dropped from a spoon. Fold the whipped cream into the mixture.

5. Pipe the mousse into the endive spears and garnish with a sliver of red pepper.

Gazpacho Andalusia

MAKES 32 SERVINGS (2 FL OZ EACH)

ELECT THE best tomatoes when making gazpacho; their flavor will make or break this classic soup. Serve it in bite-size cups made of cucumbers or in small (1- to 2-fl oz) glasses.

12 oz tomatoes, cored and diced

10 oz cucumbers, peeled and diced

4 oz green peppers, diced

4 oz red peppers, diced

10 oz crustless white bread, diced

1½ cups tomato juice

8 oz onions, sliced

2 Tbsp tomato purée

2 garlic cloves, mashed

½ tsp minced jalapeño

2 Tbsp olive oil

¼ cup white wine vinegar

2 cups water

¼ cup sugar

2 limes, zest grated

¼ cup lime juice

1 tsp salt

½ tsp ground black pepper

GARNISH

croutons

1. Reserve about ¼ cup each of the tomatoes, cucumbers, peppers, and onions for garnish.

2. Soak the bread in the tomato juice in a bowl.

3. Place the soaked bread mixture in a food processor. Purée with the diced vegetables, tomato purée, garlic, jalapeño, olive oil, and vinegar. Pour into a bowl. Stir in the water, sugar, and lime zest and juice.

4. Season the soup with salt and pepper; cover and refrigerate until chilled.

5. Serve the soup with a garnish of the reserved diced vegetables and croutons on the side.

Cold Roasted Tomato and Basil Soup

*I*F IT's hard to find yellow tomatoes for the garnish, replace them with homemade or jarred roasted yellow peppers. Serve this delicious soup already portioned in small (2- to 3-fl oz) glasses as hors d'oeuvre, or as appetizers in cups made of hollowed-out tomatoes.

4 garlic cloves, minced

1 Tbsp olive oil

½ lb celery, chopped

5 medium onions, chopped

1 cup chopped leeks, white part only

1½ lb plum tomatoes, roasted

1 qt vegetable stock

½ bunch basil

1 bay leaf

½ tsp salt

pinch of ground black pepper

GARNISH

1 lb yellow tomatoes, diced

½ cup basil chiffonade

1. Lightly sauté the garlic in the oil in a large saucepan.

2. Add the celery, onions, and leeks and sauté until they are fragrant.

3. Add the tomatoes, stock, basil, and bay leaves. Simmer until the vegetables are tender, about 40 minutes.

4. Remove the bay leaves and purée the soup, in batches, in a blender; season with salt and pepper. Pour the soup into a large storage container, cover, and refrigerate until cold.

5. Adjust seasoning before serving, if necessary. Garnish with diced tomatoes and basil chiffonade.

ROASTING PEPPERS

To roast peppers, place the whole peppers under the broiler or over an open flame, and cook on all sides, turning them every couple of minutes so they get an even char.

Remove them from the broiler or stove top, place them in a paper bag, and roll down the top to seal it (the trapped steam will help to separate the skin from the flesh). When the peppers are cool enough to handle, remove them from the bag, peel away the skin (it should fall off easily just by gently rubbing), remove the seeds, and rinse the flesh briefly under cool water.

Cold Tomato and Zucchini Soup

*T*HIS SOUP is always a crowd pleaser, but make it extra special by garnishing with a dollup of sour cream seasoned with a sprinkling of salt and a dash of lime zest.

1¼ pounds plum tomatoes, peeled, seeded, and coarsely chopped, about 4 cups

2 cups tomato juice

1 small onion, coarsely chopped

1 red pepper, seeded, deribbed, and coarsely chopped

½ cucumber, peeled, seeded, and coarsely chopped

½ zucchini, coarsely chopped

¼ cup chopped cilantro

¼ cup chopped basil

¼ cup chopped parsley

1½ tablespoons drained, prepared horseradish

1 tablespoon red wine vinegar

3 garlic cloves, chopped

chicken broth, as needed

Tabasco, to taste

salt as needed

ground black pepper as needed

1. Combine all the ingredients, except the broth, Tabasco, salt, and pepper, in a blender or food processor, working in small batches if necessary.

2. Process the soup in short pulses to a coarse purée. If the soup is too thick, adjust the consistency with some chicken broth. Add the Tabasco, salt, and pepper to taste.

3. Serve in 2- to 3-fluid ounce glasses, or in cucumber segments hollowed out to make uniform small cups.

Chapter Three

FILLINGS, DIPS,
AND TOPPINGS

I F A CONTAINER or base can be thought of as the backbone of an hors d'oeuvre, then a filling, dip, or topping could be considered its heart because it supplies the pulse, its flavor. Whether they are complex mixtures of fruits, vegetables, grains, meats, and dairy products or a single, well-chosen ingredient, the fillings, dips, and toppings at a party are always at the center of conversation-sparking hors d'oeuvre.

Fillings, dips, and toppings are some of the easiest things to prepare and most of them can be made ahead of time and stored for at least a few days. Favorite condiments can be an ingredient in a dip or filling, or used as is. Mustard, for example, is no stranger to the hors d'oevure table as a dipping sauce for pretzels, and a sweet fruit chutney, relish, or compote is an easy flavoring dab on meats or cheeses. Flavored oils can add a glorious trail across or a ring of dots around a plain goat's milk cheese on a contrasting-color plate.

Jarred or homemade fillings, dips, and toppings, such as hummus or tapenade, can be ingredients themselves, such as the spread for vegetable tea sandwiches or miniature open-face sandwiches topped with micro-greens or sprouts.

Even just a few fillings, dips, and toppings mounded in attractive bowls or ramekins can liven up any spread. Present them in various ways to enliven or dress up a table. For example, when making Dilled Salmon Rillettes (page 56), rather than spooning them into a serving crock, use a pastry bag and star tip to pipe rosettes of the mixture onto rye toast points and garnish with a pluche of dill. Use contrasting colors to make a simpler but equally dramatic platter:

serve Pork Piccadillo Empanadas (page 75) with the Papaya and Black Bean Salsa (page 39) to create a lively look and flavor combination.

Sometimes a single food, such as fondue, can be the focal point of your table. Fondue has strong traditions and its particular style and equipment for serving and presentation create a beautiful display.

Fondue originated in 18th-century Switzerland and is still enjoyed there by natives and tourists alike. Each canton claims its own distinct combination of cheeses and other local ingredients that range from garlic to mushrooms to dry cider to be the classic version. The most common fondue contains both Gruyère and Emmentaler cheeses, a combination that gives the mixture a nearly perfect, smooth, yet full-bodied flavor. The addition of a dry white wine helps to buffer the cheese from the heat, preventing it from scorching in the serving pot, which is set over the direct heat of a warming plate or open flame.

Fondue combinations are nearly endless. Experiment with cheeses and flavors, such as chiles, cilantro, and Jack cheese for a Mexican flair or roasted garlic, oregano, and parsley for a more Italian flavor profile.

Although the recipe for fondue adapts to individual tastes, the ritual of eating it does not. A traditional fondue is shared communally by family and guests, who spear a solitary piece of bread, meat, seafood, vegetables, or other item on a long-handled fork, dip it in the melted cheese, and spin the cheese around the food to coat it. With the fork held in the pot but out of the cheese, the cheese can drip and cool a bit before it is carefully bitten off of the skewer. The trick and etiquette is to make sure the fork, which goes back into the cheese mixture, does not touch the mouth in the process of biting.

This same dipping and eating procedure applies to dessert fondue, which calls for cubes of toasted cake or pieces of fruit to be dipped into a cream and melted chocolate mixture.

FLAVORED OILS AND VINEGARS

Good-quality oils and vinegars can be infused with spices, aromatics, herbs, and fruits or vegetables to expand their uses. They work well as condiments, drizzled in lines and swirls or as droplets to add a bit of intense flavor and color to a plate or platter of hors d'oeuvre, or as a dip for a bit of crusty bread. Flavored oils and vinegars make excellent dressings for vegetables, pastas, grains, or fruits. And, as with most oils and vinegars, they are well suited to add to vinaigrettes and other dressings, but their flavors and colors produce special effects.

Although commercially prepared versions of flavored oils are shelf-stable, it is essential to store homemade varieties that contain fresh or raw ingredients, especially raw garlic or shallots, in the refrigerator for only a short time to prevent toxic bacterial growth and cause food-borne illnesses. Make small quantities of these oils and use them within a few days to be sure that they are safe to use and will have the best flavor and color.

To infuse oils and vinegars, use one of the following four methods:

METHOD 1: A WARM INFUSION

Heat the oil or vinegar very gently in a saucepan over low heat with flavoring ingredients, such as citrus zest, just until fragrant. Let the oil or vinegar steep off the heat with the flavoring ingredients until cool and pour into storage bottles or containers. You can strain the oil or vinegar for a clearer final product or leave the flavoring ingredients in for a more intense flavor.

METHOD 2: STEEPING

Place herbs or other aromatics in a glass or plastic bottle. Heat the oil or vinegar briefly, just until warm, pour it over the aromatics, and let the infusion rest until the desired flavor is achieved. Add fresh aromatics after the oil or vinegar has steeped for several days for an even more intense flavor.

METHOD 3: PURÉES

Purée raw, blanched, or fully cooked vegetables, herbs, or fruits, pour into a saucepan, and bring to a simmer. If necessary, simmer the purée a few minutes to reduce the liquid and concentrate the flavors. Add the oil or vinegar and transfer to a storage container. Leave the oil as is, and use it as a purée, or strain it to remove the fiber and pulp.

METHOD 4: COLD INFUSION

Combine room-temperature oil with ground spices in a bowl or pitcher and pour the mixture into a storage container. Let the mixture stand until the vinegar or oil is clear and the spices have settled in the bottom of the container. Carefully decant the vinegar or oil once the desired flavor is reached.

Papaya and Black Bean Salsa

MAKES 16 SERVINGS (32 FL OZ)

THE UNUSUAL combination of papaya and black beans is not only delicious, but looks beautiful, especially in combination with the red of the pepper and greens of the jalapeños and cilantro. Serve this salsa as a dip with chips and sour cream, or in small cups (2 to 4 fl oz) as a bite-size salad.

1 cup cooked black beans, rinsed
    and drained

1 ripe papaya, cut into small dice

2 red peppers, cut into small dice

1 red onion, cut into small dice

2 jalapeños, minced

3 Tbsp chopped cilantro

2 tsp dried Mexican oregano

3 Tbsp minced fresh ginger

¼ cup olive oil

2 limes, juiced

1 tsp ground black pepper

2 tsp kosher salt

1. Combine all ingredients and adjust seasoning.
2. Cover and refrigerate if not serving immediately.

MANGO PREPARATION

Mango is a sweet fruit with a creamy texture. It is an excellent substitute for papaya in many recipes, including the Papaya and Black Bean Salsa.

To prepare a mango, cut the fruit off of the seed in four sections. Run a knife along the bottom of the two thinner sections to remove the fruit from the skin. Cut the two larger sections in half and then remove the fruit in the same way.

Another method involves cutting the two larger half sections in a crosshatch pattern. This will divide the fruit into cubes. Be sure to cut only through the fruit and not through the skin of the mango.

Next, bend back the mango half so that the cubed pieces pop up. The mango cubes can then be easily cut from the skin with a knife.

AT LEFT: *Salsa Fresca (back), Tomatillo Salsa (middle), and Papaya and Black Bean Salsa (front)*

Tomatillo Salsa

USING TOMATILLOS rather than tomatoes for salsa adds a fresh and bright citrusy flavor. The cilantro is also an integral flavor in this recipe—there is no substitute.

1 lb 4 oz tomatillos

1 large jalapeño

4 large garlic cloves, bruised

1 cup water

salt to taste

1 bunch cilantro

ground black pepper to taste

1. Cut the tomatillos into wedges and place in a saucepan with the jalapeño, garlic, and water.

2. Cover the mixture and bring to a boil over medium heat, reduce to a simmer, and cook until the tomatillos are olive green in color, about 20 minutes.

3. Put the tomatillo mixture into a food processor and process until fully blended. Taste the mixture and adjust the seasonings with salt if needed.

4. Add the cilantro to the processor and pulse to chop and combine with the salsa. Season with salt and pepper.

TOMATILLOS

In appearance, tomatillos resemble small green tomatoes enclosed in a papery husk. They have a tart flavor and a crisp texture.

Tomatillos are used fresh in salads and in many Mexican and South American salsas. Cooking tomatillos brings out more of their flavor and their sturdy texture helps them keep their shape. Roast tomatillos with garlic and herbs for a unique side dish.

Tomatillos are mainly produced in warm climates with long growing seasons. This means they are available in grocery stores at most times of the year. Tomatillos can be stored in a cool, dark place or they can be frozen whole or sliced.

Salsa Fresca

MAKES 16 SERVINGS (32 FL OZ)

USE THIS classic salsa it to make nachos. Simply spread corn chips in a ovenproof pan, sprinkle with grated Cheddar and Jack cheeses and a selection of toppings—sliced black olives, refried beans, and finely chopped jalapeños are excellent choices. Top with some salsa and bake in a preheated 400°F oven until the cheese is fully melted, about 10 minutes.

1 lb 2 oz tomatoes, seeded and diced

½ cup minced onion

1 green pepper, diced

2 garlic cloves, minced

1 Tbsp chopped cilantro

1 tsp chopped oregano

2 limes, juiced

1 jalapeño, minced

2 Tbsp olive oil

salt and pepper to taste

Combine all ingredients, taste, and adjust seasoning. Refrigerate leftovers.

WORKING WITH HOT PEPPERS

When working with hot peppers, such as habaneros, there are a few safety precautions that should be taken. Hot peppers can burn skin, so wear rubber gloves while cutting them. However, latex gloves do not protect your hands because capsaicin, the compound that makes peppers hot, can pass through latex. Avoid touching your face while you are preparing hot peppers and watch out for spraying oils when you cut into the pepper. These oils can irritate or burn skin.

The majority of a pepper's heat is found in the interior veins and in the seeds because they have come into close contact with the veins. When preparing a dish with hot peppers, remove the seeds and veins if you wish to make the dish milder.

Chipotle Pico de Gallo

MAKES 16 SERVINGS (32 FL OZ)

*T*HE SMOKINESS of the chipotles in adobo sauce gives this salsa full-bodied flavor. This mixture is available canned—look for it in the international foods aisle in your favorite market or local bodega.

1 lb 2 oz plum tomatoes, seeded and chopped

1 cup chopped red onion

¼ cup lime juice

1½ tsp minced garlic

2 tsp chipotle in adobo sauce, mashed to a paste

salt to taste

ground black pepper to taste

¼ cup chopped cilantro

1. Combine the tomatoes, onion, lime juice, garlic, and chipotle in a bowl. Taste and season with salt and pepper. Cover and refrigerate at least 4 or up to 24 hours before serving.

2. Mix the chopped cilantro into the pico de gallo just before serving.

CHIPOTLES

Chipotles are smoked jalapeños and can be purchased either dried, pickled, or canned in adobo sauce. Adobo sauce is a deep red sauce made from chiles, spices, herbs, and vinegar.

Chipotles are medium-heat chiles with a rich smoky flavor. They are often used to flavor soups, sauces, salsas, stew, and even desserts. Chipotles' smokiness is ideal for barbeque sauces and meat marinades.

Salsa Verde

THE UNUSUAL mix of herbs and spices makes this salsa refreshingly different. Omit the anchovy fillets and serve the salsa as a colorful topping for a smoked salmon canapé.

2 shallots, finely diced

¼ cup red wine vinegar

salt to taste

4 salt-packed anchovies

1 cup chopped flat-leaf parsley

¼ cup chopped chives

2 Tbsp chopped chervil

2 Tbsp chopped thyme

3 Tbsp chopped capers

1 Tbsp finely chopped lemon zest

1¼ cup extra-virgin olive oil

1. Cover the shallots with the vinegar in a small bowl and season with salt. Let them macerate for about 20 minutes.

2. Rinse the anchovies well and remove their fins and backbones. Finely chop the fillets and place in a medium bowl.

3. Add the chopped herbs, capers, lemon zest, and olive oils to the anchovies and stir to a sauce-like consistency. Add the shallots and vinegar. Adjust seasoning.

4. Transfer the salsa to a clean storage container. Refrigerate immediately.

Hummus

MAKES 32 SERVINGS

THIS POPULAR Middle Eastern dip is a staple in an hors d'oeuvre repertoire. Experiment with the amount of tahini (sesame seed paste) in the hummus—using more or less makes a great difference in both flavor and texture. Use roasted garlic instead of fresh for a softer flavor.

1 lb 8 oz cooked chickpeas, drained

½ cup tahini (sesame seed paste)

3 Tbsp lemon juice or to taste

¼ cup olive oil

4 garlic cloves, minced

1 Tbsp salt

ground black pepper to taste

1. Combine all the ingredients in the bowl of a food processor.

2. Purée the ingredients (in batches if necessary), adding water to thin if needed.

3. Adjust seasoning with lemon juice and garlic.

NOTE: Hummus can be passed through a sieve for a smoother texture.

HUMMUS

Hummus, a mixture of puréed chickpeas and tahini, is an excellent base for many ingredients. Roasted red peppers, curry powder, roasted garlic, cooked spinach and feta, sun-dried tomatoes, olives, jalapeños, or cooked beets can be added to a basic hummus recipe to create a variety of delicious dips for flatbreads and vegetables. Hummus also works very well as a sandwich spread with roasted vegetables and deli meats.

AT RIGHT: Baba Ganoush (back, page 46) and
Hummus (front) with toasted pita wedges

Roasted Eggplant Dip with Mint
(Baba Ghanoush)

MAKES 32 SERVINGS (32 FL OZ)

*H*ARISSA, NOT a typical ingredient in baba ghanoush, is a North African condiment made of chiles, garlic, spices, and oil. It adds a welcome and unusual depth of flavor to this classic dip.

4 lb eggplants, cut in half lengthwise

3 tsp salt

2 tsp ground black pepper

¼ cup olive oil plus extra for brushing eggplant

3 shallots, minced

6 Tbsp lemon juice

½ cup tahini (sesame seed paste)

¼ cup chopped flat-leaf parsley leaves

⅓ cup chopped mint

2 garlic cloves, minced

Harissa to taste (recipe follows)

1. Season the eggplant with 1 teaspoon of the salt and 1 teaspoon of the pepper and lightly coat the cut faces with some of the olive oil. Roast cut side down on a sheet pan in a preheated 375°F oven until soft, 30 to 40 minutes. Cool to room temperature; scoop out flesh and discard seeds.

2. While the eggplant is roasting, macerate the shallots in the lemon juice with ¼ tsp salt.

3. Combine the roasted eggplant with ¼ cup olive oil, the macerated shallots, tahini, and parsley.

4. Season the eggplant mixture with the mint, garlic, the remaining salt and pepper, and harissa. Chop to a rough texture by hand or purée in a food processor until smooth.

HARISSA

MAKES: 2 CUPS

THIS PASTE will add an extra dimension of flavor to almost any recipe, from vinaigrettes to beans.

10 jalapeños, roasted, peeled, and seeded

4 red peppers, roasted, peeled, and seeded

1 Tbsp whole cumin seeds, toasted and ground

1 Tbsp puréed garlic

3 Tbsp hot Hungarian paprika

1½ tsp cayenne

¾ cup olive oil

3 Tbsp lemon juice
salt to taste

1. Combine the jalapeños, peppers, cumin, garlic paste, paprika, and cayenne in a blender. Grind to a paste-like consistency.

2. Remove the paste to a bowl. Slowly whisk in the oil to create a smooth sauce. Add the lemon juice and salt.

3. Transfer to a storage container.

STORAGE: Cover and refrigerate leftovers; they will keep up to 2 weeks.

Tapenade

MAKES 32 SERVINGS: (32 FL OZ)

*A*NCHOVY FILLETS are optional in this recipe—replace with fresh herbs, such as oregano or basil, or more robust ingredients, such as grated Parmesan cheese, mustard, or hot peppers.

12 oz Niçoise olives, pitted

8 oz black olives, pitted

4 oz salt-packed anchovy fillets, rinsed and dried

⅓ cup capers, rinsed

6 garlic cloves, minced

ground black pepper to taste

lemon juice to taste

olive oil to taste

chopped herbs, such as oregano or basil, to taste

1. In a food processor, combine the olives, anchovies, capers, garlic, and pepper. With the motor running, slowly pour in the lemon juice and oil through the feed tube. Blend until chunky and easily spread, but do not overmix; the tapenade should have texture and identifiable bits of olive.

2. Adjust seasoning and finish with the herbs.

USES FOR TAPENADE

Tapenade has many uses as an ingredient in both hors d'oeuvre and in main entrées:

- *Spread tapenade on garlic crostinis as a canapé.*

- *Prepare a fresh tomato salad with tapenade and vinaigrette dressing.*

- *Serve tapenade with roasted lamb.*

- *Serve tapenade with poached salmon.*

- *Spread tapenade on foccacia or French bread for gourmet sandwiches.*

- *Prepare smoked salmon and tapenade canapés.*

- *Toss tapenade with cooked pasta, chicken, and vegetables.*

- *Top homemade tomato or vegetable soup with a dollop of tapenade.*

Eggplant Caponata

MAKES 3 CUPS

W) HILE THIS eggplant caponata is lovely served on rounds of toasted bread or on crostinis, a unique presentation is to serve it unaccompanied on individual spoons for the guests to discover the hors d'oeuvre's complex flavors.

¼ cup olive oil plus as needed

½ lb eggplant, cut into ¼-in dice

2 minced garlic cloves

1 red pepper, cut into ¼-in dice

1 yellow onion, cut into ¼-in dice

3 oz diced green olives

4 canned plum tomatoes, seeded, cut into ¼-in dice

2 Tbsp drained capers

2 Tbsp sugar

⅓ cup white wine vinegar

1 Tbsp shredded basil

1 piece (about 4 oz) Parmigiano-Reggiano, cut into thin shavings (use a vegetable peeler)

1. Heat 6 tablespoons of olive oil in a sauté pan over medium heat, add the eggplant, and sauté until lightly browned and tender, about 5 minutes. Add the garlic and sauté for 30 seconds; drain the eggplant on a sheet pan lined with paper towels. Scrape into a large bowl.

2. Heat 1 tablespoon of olive oil in the same pan and sauté the peppers and onions until tender, about 5 minutes. Add to the eggplant and place in a bowl.

3. Heat 1 tablespoon of olive oil in the same pan and sauté the green olives for one minute. Add the tomatoes and the capers, and cook for another minute. Add the sugar and the vinegar, and cook, reducing the liquid for 1 minute. Add to the eggplant mixture, mix well, and sprinkle with the basil. Add more olive oil if desired.

4. Serve the caponata on individual spoons and garnish with a thin strip of Parmigiano-Reggiano on top.

Eggplant Caviar

HILE THERE are no fish eggs in this recipe, the result is as sophisticated as caviar and makes a delicious topping for crostinis brushed with garlic and extra-virgin olive oil.

3 large eggplants

8 to 10 Tbsp extra-virgin olive oil

1 tsp kosher salt

½ tsp freshly ground pepper

6 garlic cloves, unpeeled

2 red peppers

8 oz shiitake mushrooms, stemmed and sliced

1. Slice the eggplants in half lengthwise, then, without cutting the skins, score the flesh in a crosshatch pattern.

2. Sprinkle the eggplants with about 1 Tbsp olive oil, 1 tsp salt, and ½ tsp pepper and place, cut side up, on a sheet pan. Wrap the garlic in aluminum foil and roast the eggplant and garlic in a preheated 500°F oven for 25 minutes.

3. Remove the foil from the eggplants and check the garlic. If the garlic is soft, remove it from the oven, otherwise continue roasting both the wrapped garlic and the uncovered eggplants. The eggplants are done when they are soft and golden, about 30 minutes more.

4. Char the peppers on all sides over an open flame. Place in a brown paper bag or plastic container, seal, and let steam until cool enough to handle. Gently scrape away the charred skin, discard the stem and seeds, and cut out the veins. Dice the pepper and set aside.

5. Sauté the mushrooms in 2 tablespoons of olive oil for 2 minutes over high heat. The mushrooms should be soft and lightly browned.

6. Place all ingredients in the bowl of a food processor fitted with the metal chopping blade and process until smooth. Add more olive oil if desired.

7. Serve immediately, or cover and refrigerate for up to 3 days.

Bagna Cauda

MAKES 2 CUPS

B AGNA CAUDA, a warm dip originating from the Piedmonte region of Italy, can be served with raw and cooked vegetables, flatbreads, crostinis, and sliced artisan breads.

1 cup extra-virgin olive oil

5 Tbsp minced garlic

½ cup (1 stick) unsalted butter, cut into pieces

8 to 10 anchovy fillets, chopped

½ tsp fresh lemon juice

½ tsp grated lemon zest

¼ tsp kosher salt

⅛ tsp freshly ground black pepper

vegetables or bread for dipping

1. Heat ¼ cup of the oil over medium heat in a small sauce pot. Add the garlic and cook until fragrant and soft, about 1 minute. Add the remaining ¾ cup oil and the butter and cook gently, stirring, to melt the butter. Lower the heat, add the anchovies, and cook until they dissolve, about 3 minutes.

2. Remove the pan from the heat and stir in the lemon juice and zest. Season with the salt and pepper.

3. Transfer the bagna cauda to an earthenware or fondue pot with a flame underneath, place in the middle of a platter, and surround with desired vegetables or bread. Serve immediately.

Caramelized Onion Dip
with Pommes Frites

MAKES 2 CUPS

*T*HIS RECIPE takes a much loved combination, onion dip and potato chips, and transforms it into a more sophisticated hors d'oeuvre that can be served at a casual luncheon or a formal dinner party.

1 Tbsp vegetable oil plus extra for frying, about 24 fl oz

1 medium onion, quartered and thinly sliced

2 tsp chopped sage leaves

1 cup sour cream

½ cup mayonnaise

1 tsp salt, divided, or to taste

1 tsp freshly ground pepper, divided, or to taste

1 green onion, sliced thinly on the bias (sliced crosswise on the diagonal)

2 lb Idaho potatoes, thinly sliced into rounds

1. Heat 1 Tbsp of the oil in heavy medium saucepan over medium-low heat. Add the onions and sage. Cover and cook until the onions are deep golden brown, stirring occasionally, about 30 minutes. Remove from the heat and let cool.

2. Whisk together sour cream and mayonnaise in a medium bowl to blend. Stir in the cooled caramelized onions and season with ½ tsp salt and ½ tsp pepper. Top with sliced green onions and set aside.

3. Preheat 2 in of oil to 325°F in a deep saucepan. Pat potato slices with paper towels and fry a few at a time in the oil until crisp, removing each batch of fried potatoes with a slotted spoon to a plate lined with paper towels. Season each batch immediately with the remaining salt and pepper and repeat with the remaining potatoes. Serve immediately.

Crabmeat and Camembert Dip

MAKES 4 TO 6 SERVINGS

CAMEMBERT IS a creamy, fairly mild cheese that compliments the sweetness of the crabmeat. Brie, although a firmer cheese, would be an appropriate substitute for the Camembert.

¼ cup olive oil

1 minced medium shallot

1 cup heavy cream

1 cup milk

8 oz Camembert, trimmed of rind

1 tsp kosher salt

½ tsp freshly ground white pepper

1 lb lump crabmeat, picked clean of shells and cartilage

1 Tbsp chopped parsley

2 to 3 Tbsp Tomato Marmalade (recipe follows)

French bread, cut into ¼-in-thick slices, for dipping

1. Heat the olive oil in a saucepan over medium heat, add the shallots, and cook, stirring occasionally, until the shallots are soft and translucent, about 3 minutes. Add the heavy cream and milk and bring to a simmer. Add the Camembert, salt, and pepper and whisk until the cheese melts into the cream. Add the crabmeat.

2. Cook over medium heat until the cream is slightly reduced, about 10 minutes. Remove the pan from the heat and stir in the parsley. Transfer the dip to a fondue pot and stir in 2 to 3 Tbsp of the Tomato Marmalade. Serve warm with French bread.

TOMATO MARMALADE

MAKES ABOUT ¾ CUP

SIMILAR TO a tomato sauce, this is a purée of fresh tomatoes, garlic, olive oil, and herbs. Tomato marmalade is excellent for drizzling on soups, dips, canapés, and crostinis.

8 oz Roma tomatoes, cored, halved, and seeded

½ tsp kosher salt

1 thinly sliced garlic clove

2½ cups olive oil

1 tsp chopped oregano

1. Place the tomatoes in a small saucepan and season with the salt. Add the garlic and enough olive oil to barely cover the tops of the tomatoes.

2. Bring the oil to a very low simmer and cook for about 1 hour. Remove the tomatoes from the oil with a slotted spoon and place in a food processor. Pulse until smooth and add the oregano. Use immediately or cover and refrigerate for up to 1 week.

Curry Dip

A N EXCELLENT alternative to hummus, this dip is delicious with fresh vegetables, flatbreads, and sliced artisan breads.

¾ cup mayonnaise

¼ cup sour cream

2 Tbsp grated onion

1 Tbsp fresh lemon juice

1 tsp curry powder

1 tsp grated lemon zest

1 tsp minced garlic

vegetables for dipping

Combine all ingredients in a small bowl and mix well. Cover with plastic wrap and chill. Serve the curry dip in ramekins with assorted vegetables for dipping.

CREATIVE DIP CONTAINERS

To make an already beautiful hors d'oeuvre table more striking, be creative with what you use as the containers for dips and spreads. Hollowed-out breads and vegetables make excellent containers that will add color and interest to any display. Select a bread or vegetable of the appropriate size to accommodate the volume of your recipe; an overflowing container makes it difficult for guests to help themselves, and a container that isn't quite full looks unappealing. Vegetables commonly used as containers for dips and spreads include small red cabbages, onions, tomatoes, artichokes, and eggplants.

Cheese Fondue

*I*N ADDITION to bread cubes, other items good for dipping into the fondue include cooked and peeled baby, new, or fingerling potatoes; broccoli and cauliflower florets, cooked al dente; and whole cherry or grape tomatoes.

1 garlic clove, halved

1 cup dry white wine

8 oz Emmentaler cheese, grated

1 lb Gruyère cheese, grated

2 Tbsp cornstarch

¼ cup Kirsch

Tabasco sauce to taste

salt to taste

ground white pepper to taste

grated nutmeg to taste

2 baguettes, cubed

1. Rub the inside of an earthenware casserole with the halved garlic clove.

2. Add the wine and place the casserole over a flame.

3. When bubbles rise to the wine's surface, gradually add the cheeses, stirring constantly with a wooden spoon until the cheeses melt.

4. Dissolve the cornstarch in the Kirsch. Stirring constantly, add the Kirsch slowly to the cheese mixture.

5. Season the mixture to taste with the Tabasco, salt, pepper, and nutmeg.

6. To serve, place the casserole over a flame just high enough to keep fondue bubbling gently. Using long-handled fondue forks, dip the bread into the melted cheese.

AT RIGHT: A traditional Swiss Fondue, served with bread cubes, cornichons, and pearl onions

Dilled Salmon Rillettes

MAKES 16 SERVINGS

*T*HE BRIGHT yet delicate flavor of this preparation makes it an excellent choice to serve with spring and summertime flavors, such as fresh green salads, crisp cool beverages, and light crackers or toast points. When preparing the mixture, place it in beautiful molds for serving. Once the rillette mixture sets, it cannot be transferred to another container without destroying the smooth top and texture.

1 cup (2 sticks) butter

1 lb skinless salmon fillet, cut into
   1-in cubes

¾ cup dry white wine

¼ cup minced shallots

2 tsp salt

¼ tsp ground white pepper

3 dill sprigs, minced

1 tsp finely chopped lemon zest

1. Melt the butter in a saucepan over low heat.

2. Add the salmon, wine, shallots, salt, pepper, dill, and lemon zest; simmer slowly over very low heat, until the salmon is fully cooked, 15 to 20 minutes.

3. Remove the pan from the heat and cool until the butter begins to solidify.

4. Transfer the mixture to a chilled mixer bowl. Mix on medium speed with a paddle attachment until a smooth paste is formed.

5. Test for appropriate seasoning and consistency. Make any adjustments before placing in molds.

6. Fill desired molds, cover, and refrigerate until needed.

Pork Rillettes

SERVE THESE or any rillettes displayed in beautiful ramekins on a pâté or cheese platter to serve as a spread for crackers or a sliced baguette. The delicate flavor of the rillettes complements almost any offering of hors d'oeuvre.

2 lb boneless very fatty pork butt, cubed

1 lb mirepoix (an equal mix of carrots, onions, and celery, cut into large dice)

Standard sachet d'épices (see Note)

3 qt white beef stock

2½ Tbsp salt

2 tsp ground black pepper or more to taste

1. Place the pork, mirepoix, and sachet in a saucepan. Add stock almost to cover.

2. Simmer, covered, very slowly on the stove, or braise in a preheated 350°F oven until the meat is cooked and very tender, at least 2 hours.

3. Lift out the pork, reserving the stock and rendered fat. Discard the mirepoix and sachet. Let the meat cool slightly.

4. Transfer the meat to a chilled mixer bowl. Add the salt and pepper and mix on low speed until the meat breaks into pieces. Test for appropriate seasoning and consistency, adjusting the consistency by adding as much of the rendered fat and cooking liquid to make the mixture spreadable, not runny or dry. Make adjustments before filling the mold.

5. Divide the rillettes among earthenware molds no larger than 32 fl oz. Ladle some reserved rendered fat over them, and let cool before serving.

STORAGE: Rillettes can be refrigerated for 2 to 3 weeks.

NOTE: Recipe for a standard sachet d'épices: 3 to 4 fresh parsley stems, ½ tsp fresh thyme leaves, 1 bay leaf, ½ tsp cracked peppercorns, and 1 crushed garlic clove. Place all of these ingredients in a 4-in-square piece of cheesecloth. Gather up the edges and tie with butcher's twine, leaving a long tail of string to tie to the stockpot handle.

Pommes Frites with Spiced Mayonnaise

MAKES 4 SERVINGS

THIS SNACK, or hors d'oeuvre, is a twist on French fries and mayonnaise, a combination loved by many Europeans. The flavorful, spiced mayonnaise could also replace the traditional condiment when making sandwiches or chicken salad.

SPICED MAYONNAISE

½ cup mayonnaise

1 Tbsp white wine vinegar

½ tsp ground coriander

½ tsp ground cumin

½ tsp cayenne

¼ tsp salt

¼ tsp black pepper

POMMES FRITES

2 cups vegetable oil, preferably canola or safflower

4 russet potatoes, peeled and cut into ½-in-thick wedges

½ tsp salt

GARNISH

Chopped fresh parsley leaves

1. Put the mayonnaise in a bowl and whisk in the vinegar and spices. Transfer to a small serving bowl and set aside.

2. Heat the oil over high heat in a large, heavy pot until it reaches 375°F.

3. Carefully place half of the potatoes into the oil and cook until golden brown, about 12 minutes. Remove the potatoes with a slotted metal spoon and drain on paper towels. Immediately season the potatoes generously with salt and sprinkle with parsley. Serve the first batch with the spiced mayonnaise and repeat the frying process for the second batch of potatoes.

Pumpkin Chutney

MAKES 4 CUPS

THIS AUTUMN spread is delicious when served with fresh or dried fruit slices, artisan breads, or flatbreads. You may substitute any hard winter squash, such as butternut, for the pumpkin in this recipe.

2 Tbsp good-quality extra-virgin olive oil

½ large sweet onion, chopped

1 minced garlic clove

1 lb pumpkin, peeled and cubed

1 lemon, juiced

1 jalapeño

½ cup raisins

½ cup golden raisins

½ cup brown sugar

½ cup apricot jam

3 Tbsp white wine vinegar

1 Tbsp sliced fresh ginger

1 tsp dry mustard

1 tsp ground cinnamon

½ tsp ground nutmeg

¼ tsp ground allspice

Dash cayenne or more to taste

1. Heat the oil in a medium saucepan. Add the onion and cook until softened, about 4 minutes. Add the garlic and cook until aromatic. Add the remaining ingredients and cover the pan.

2. Cook the chutney slowly over low heat until thick, 1 to 2 hours. Remove the chile.

NOTE: Some pumpkins are drier than others, so if using some that looks dry, add no more than ½ cup of apple cider or apple juice when adding the pumpkin to the pan.

Spicy White Bean and Avocado Dip

MAKES 2 CUPS

SIMILAR TO guacamole, this white bean and avocado dip is delicious with tortillas, flavored flatbreads, fresh vegetables, and toasted pita slices.

2 ripe avocados, pitted and peeled

½ cup drained, canned white cannellini beans

2 minced garlic cloves

1 tsp minced jalapeño

¼ cup chopped cilantro

¼ cup chopped mint

2 tsp lime juice

1 tsp olive oil

1 tsp salt

½ tsp freshly ground pepper

Place the avocados, white beans, garlic, and jalapeño in a mixing bowl. Mash with a fork until chunky. Fold in the cilantro, mint, lime juice, olive oil, salt, and pepper.

MINT

Peppermint and spearmint came to the New World via the colonists, who used them for teas, cooking, and medicines. With over thirty species of this herb (the most common being spearmint and peppermint), there are so many varieties that it is difficult to count them. All types of mint contain menthol oil, which produces the cool, clean feeling associated with eating mint. For cooking, it is best to harvest the young tender leaves; as the leaves mature, they can develop a slight bitterness. Mint is very versatile. It can be used to season savory dishes as well as desserts, or it can be used in marinades for meats and in dressings for salads of greens or grains. Mint is also used to flavor a multitude of beverages from the mint julip to mojitos to tea -- hot or iced. It is commonly used to flavor ice creams, sorbets, sherbets, jellies, chocolates, and candies. Its uses are practically endless, so add some to your herb patch as it is easy to grow and is best when used fresh.

Spinach and Artichoke Dip

MAKES 5 CUPS

SERVED WARM, this creamy spinach and artichoke dip melts in your mouth and makes a perfect fall or winter dinner party hors d'oeuvre.

¼ cup clarified butter

¼ cup all-purpose flour

2 cups milk

1 cup grated Parmesan (about 4 oz)

½ cup grated Monterey Jack cheese (about 2 oz)

1 tsp salt

¼ tsp freshly grated nutmeg

¼ tsp cayenne

2 Tbsp vegetable oil

1 cup finely diced onion

1 (10-oz) bag fresh spinach, stemmed, rinsed, and chopped

2 (15-oz) cans artichoke hearts, drained and chopped (pulse in food processor)

2 Tbsp chopped garlic

Chips, toasted pita, or sliced warm bread for serving

1. Combine the clarified butter and flour in a saucepan over medium heat. Stir the mixture until a blond roux forms.

2. Use a whisk to incorporate the milk. Bring the liquid up to a boil and reduce to a simmer. Simmer the liquid until it is thick and coats the back of a spoon, 5 to 6 minutes. Remove the sauce from the heat and stir in ½ cup of the Parmesan and the Monterey Jack cheese, salt, nutmeg, and cayenne.

3. Heat the vegetable oil over medium heat in a sauté pan. Add the onion and sauté for 2 minutes. Add the spinach and stir with a wooden spoon, coating all of the leaves with oil. If the pan gets watery, carefully pour out the water.

4. Add the artichoke hearts and garlic and sauté for 2 minutes. Remove from the heat and turn into a mixing bowl. Fold in the cheese mixture. Pour into a casserole dish and sprinkle with the remaining ½ cup Parmesan.

5. Bake the dip in a preheated 400°F oven until the top is golden brown, 10 to 15 minutes.

6. Serve the dip with chips, toasted pita, or sliced warm bread.

Smoked Salmon Mousse

U SE THIS to create an eye-catching canapé. Using a pastry bag and a star tip, pipe small rosettes of the mousse onto thin slices of cucumber and garnish each with a pluche of dill. The mousse is also delicious when piped along the length of a leaf of Belgian endive or in the center of a cracker.

1 lb 8 oz smoked salmon, diced

2 cups fish stock, cold, or 1 cup fish stock
   and 1 cup water

1 oz powdered gelatin

1 tsp salt

½ tsp ground white pepper

2 cups heavy cream, whipped to soft peaks

1. Combine the smoked salmon and 1 cup stock in a food processor and process to a smooth consistency. Push through a sieve and transfer to a bowl.

2. Sprinkle the gelatin over the remaining cold stock or water in a small bowl and stir to break up any clumps. Let the gelatin soften in the stock for about 3 minutes, until the gelatin absorbs the liquid. Heat the softened gelatin over simmering water, or in a microwave for about 20 seconds on low power, until the granules melt and the mixture is clear.

3. Blend the gelatin into the salmon mixture and season with salt and pepper.

4. Fold in the whipped cream. Spoon the mousse into ramekins or pipe onto sliced vegetables or crackers as desired. Refrigerate the mousse until firm, at least 2 hours.

Foie Gras Mousse

SERVING FOIE gras at any event instantly makes the occasion more elegant. Foie gras mousse is best enjoyed on simple toasted croutons, but it is also wonderful when embellished with other flavors; prunes soaked in Armangac and filled with this mousse is a classic combination.

1 lb 8 oz high-quality foie gras, cleaned and veins removed

2 tsp salt

½ tsp ground white pepper

¼ cup Sauternes

½ cup minced shallots

1 garlic clove, minced

½ cup (1 stick) butter

¾ cup heavy cream, whipped to medium peaks

1. Put the foie gras in a nonreactive bowl and sprinkle with the salt, pepper, and Sauternes. Toss to coat, cover with plastic wrap, and marinate overnight in the refrigerator.

2. Drain the foie gras and cut into 1-in chunks.

3. Sauté the shallots and garlic in the butter until soft; do not brown. Add the foie gras and cook over high heat, stirring, until the foie gras is cooked through, 4 to 5 minutes.

4. Cool the mixture to 90°F and purée in the bowl of a food processor. Pass the purée through a drum sieve into a bowl set over an ice bath and stir until it begins to thicken. Fold the whipped cream into the mixture and adjust seasoning.

5. Line a 2-lb terrine mold with plastic wrap, leaving an overhang. Fill with the foie gras mousse and smooth the top. Cover and refrigerate overnight before serving.

STORAGE: The mousse can be kept, covered, in the refrigerator for up to 3 days.

FOIE GRAS

Foie gras is a classic luxury food item. Foie gras is produced from both geese and ducks and is graded A, B, or C based on the size, appearance, and texture of the liver. Grade-A liver must weigh at least 1½ pounds, and it should be round and firm, with no blemishes. The best grade liver is used in terrines and pâtés.

Grade-B foie gras weighs between 1 and 1¼ pounds, has a good texture, and may not be as round. A liver weighing less than a pound, slightly flat in shape, and containing visual imperfections will receive a grade of C. Foie gras is expensive, regardless of the grade. Be certain that you get the quality you are paying for.

Duck Confit

MAKES 3½ CUPS

THIS IS an excellent duck confit and easy to prepare. It has a nice salt content and a good spice presence without overwhelming the flavor of the duck. Remove the skin before shredding the meat and using it on a canapé.

2 lb 10 oz Moulard duck legs (about 3)

3 Tbsp kosher salt

CURE MIX

2 Tbsp light brown sugar

1½ tsp quatre épices

½ tsp dry thyme leaves

1 garlic clove, minced

5 peppercorns

1 qt rendered duck fat

1 cup water

1. Remove the thigh bones from the duck legs but leave the drumstick bones in; reserve any trimmings for stock or a similar use.

2. Combine the cure mix ingredients: salt, brown sugar, quatre épices, thyme, garlic, and peppercorns. Rub the duck pieces well with the cure mixture.

3. Place the duck in a stainless-steel pan, cover, and press with a weight. Let the duck cure in this manner in the refrigerator for 2 days.

4. On the third day, rinse any remaining cure from the duck pieces and blot dry.

5. Bring the duck fat and water to a simmer; add the duck pieces and simmer for 3 hours, or until very tender.

6. Allow the duck confit to cool to room temperature in the duck fat. Cover the confit (in the fat) with plastic wrap and refrigerate. Remove the pieces of confit from the fat as needed.

STORAGE: Cover the confit with plastic wrap and store up to 5 days in the refrigerator.

NOTE: The duck fat for this recipe can be the rendered fat from duck skin and roasted ducks, or purchased duck fat. The fat from this batch of confit can be gently remelted and strained through cheesecloth. Store it, covered, in the refrigerator and it can be reused to make a second batch of confit.

Tuna Confit

*T*HIS CONFIT is best if served immediately after it is prepared. It can be refrigerated for several days, but the delicate texture will be affected. The herbed oil mixture can be refrigerated for up to a week and used to flavor salad, to make canapés, for cooking, or to prepare more tuna confit.

1½ lb tuna (steak, belly strip, or good-sized trimmings)

2 Tbsp salt

HERBED OIL

⅓ cup sliced yellow onion

4 garlic cloves, quartered lengthwise

1 fennel bulb, thinly sliced

1 serrano, split lengthwise, seeded (optional)

4 basil stems, bruised

4 thyme sprigs, bruised

4 bay leaves, crushed

1 tsp peppercorns

3 to 4 cups mild olive oil

1. Put the fish in a nonreactive bowl and sprinkle with the salt. Lightly rub it all over the fish so there is a visible coating of salt on the surface. Cover with plastic wrap and marinate small pieces in the refrigerator for 1 hour and large pieces overnight.

2. Put the herbed oil ingredients into a medium saucepan and heat to 180°F. Keep the oil hot at this temperature for 20 to 30 minutes.

3. Add the salted fish to the oil and gently poach it in the oil. Watch the fish carefully; when it is barely pink in the center, remove from the oil and place on a serving dish. Adjust the seasoning.

4. Cool the oil, strain if desired, and pour a little over the fish. Serve immediately, or cover with plastic wrap and refrigerate until ready to serve.

Chapter Four

FILLED OR STUFFED, LAYERED, AND ROLLED

VEGETABLES, BREADS, AND PREPARED DOUGH SHEETS are all common items that make ideal bases for making filled and layered hors d'oeuvre, such as stuffed mushrooms, canapés, tea sandwiches, empanadas, and wontons.

VEGETABLES

Use vegetables as both a container for stuffed hors d'oeuvre as well as the stuffing. Almost any vegetable that can be portioned as a bite-size element that can be hollowed out and filled can serve as a container to be stuffed; mushrooms, cherry tomatoes, and radishes are popular choices. Dice the trimmings and combine with other ingredients (i.e., bread crumbs, cheeses, herbs, and spices) to make a tasty filling. Other vegetation, such as brine-packed grape leaves, fresh blossoms, and dried nori (seaweed) sheets can make a sturdy, edible wrap for savory fillings.

Buy sheets of nori in neatly cut stacks the size used to roll sushi. Look closely at a sheet of nori to distinguish a shiny side and a side that has a slightly rough texture. Spread the rice and filling on the rougher side, so that after the sushi is rolled, the presentation or shiny side is displayed. Making sushi is a surprisingly quick task—the time-consuming part is the preparation of the rice and other filling ingredients, which can be done up to a day before serving. It is not advisable to make the rolls too far in advance; the nori will lose its appealing crispness and the other ingredients will lose the freshness that is the joy of the delicious rolls.

SANDWICHES

There are practically unlimited ingredient combinations for making delicious and attractive sandwich hors d'oeuvre, a category that includes canapés and finger and tea sandwiches, which are sandwiches usually cut into small, special shapes eaten in one or two bites. A closed sandwich includes both top and bottom slices of bread; sandwiches with only one slice of bread as a base are known as open or open-face sandwiches. Canapés are small, open-face sandwiches; the word *canapé* is French for "couch." The small base of toast, usually cut out with a shaped cutter, provides a cushion on which any number of toppings can gather. Any sandwich needs some sort of coating, such as plain or flavored butter, spreadable cheese, or mayonnaise to act as a moisture barrier so that filling or topping does not make the bread soggy. The spread also can serve as "glue" that holds the sandwich together.

SANDWICHES AS ART

Finger and tea sandwiches are delicate items made on fine-grained breads that are trimmed of their crusts and precisely cut into shapes and sizes.

To prepare finger and tea sandwiches, it is best to start with a large uncut loaf of bread. Trim off the crusts and thinly slice the bread lengthwise to make a large surface area for the filling. Coat the bread with a spread or filling. For open-face sandwiches, add a garnish and cut out the sandwiches; for closed sandwiches, cover with another slice of bread (or make a stack with a different filling on each slice of bread), cut to shape, and serve immediately.

It is most efficient (in terms of supplies and food cost) to cut sandwiches into straight-edged shapes such as squares, rectangles, diamonds, or triangles. Rounds, ovals, and other special shapes can be visually appealing and are achieved using cutters in various shapes. However, the yield is generally lower in preparing these shapes.

The shapes should be uniform so they will offer the best presentation when arranged on trays or plates. Cut tea sandwiches as close to serving time as possible. To hold sandwiches that have been prepared ahead of time, use airtight containers or cover with damp cloths.

AT LEFT: *Egg Salad Tea Sandwiches (back, page 87) and Smoked Salmon Tea Sandwiches (front, page 79)*

AT RIGHT: *Fried Wontons with Mustard Sauce (page 76)*

BREADS

Breads for making tea sandwiches and canapé bases run a fairly wide gamut, including many ethnic specialties. Sliced white and wheat Pullman loaves are used to make many cold tea sandwiches, but rye and multigrain are excellent choices as well. The tight crumb of a good Pullman makes it a good choice for delicate tea and finger sandwiches, since they must be sliced thinly without crumbling.

Flatbreads can be cut and toasted in the oven to be used as bases for canapés or as chips or crackers for dips and spreads. Tortillas are a classic example. They can be used to create wraps or melty, delicious quesadillas with any number of fillings or cut into wedges or strips and baked or fried for use (depending on size) as chips or a crisp garnish for a canapé.

Both the flavor and texture characteristics of breads for an hors d'oeuvre sandwich selection are important considerations. Bread should be firm enough and thick enough to hold the filling, but not so thick that the sandwich is too dry to enjoy.

Most breads can be sliced in advance of sandwich preparation as long as they are carefully covered to prevent drying. Some sandwiches call for toasted bread, which should be done immediately before assembling the sandwich.

Bread choices include:

- *Pullman loaves of white, wheat, or rye.*

- *Flatbreads, including pita and lavash.*

- *Flour and corn tortillas.*

DOUGHS AND BATTERS

Doughs are used to make filled dumplings, such as empanadas or wontons, and can be made fresh or purchased already rolled and portioned, as are wonton wrappers and phyllo dough. Both phyllo and wonton dough are rolled very thin and thus will dry quickly when exposed to the air. To keep these doughs pliable, so that they do not become brittle while being stuffed and sealed, keep the main portion under plastic wrap covered with a damp towel while working with one piece at a time.

Dumpling doughs, like those used for empanadas, are simple to make, even for the novice—so give them a try. Empanada dough is made at the same time as the filling. It is a soft dough that cannot be rolled, cut, and stored for later use, as can wonton wrappers.

Crêpe batter is a thin pancake batter that is also easy to make. Crêpe batter may be made a day or two ahead of time, covered, and stored in the refrigerator. Crêpes may be cooked ahead of time, layered with parchment or wax paper between them and held at room temperature for up to 2 hours. For longer storage, wrap them tightly in plastic wrap and store in the refrigerator for a day or two before they are filled or they can be frozen.

Deviled Eggs

THIS IS A CLASSIC and always favorite hors d'oeuvre—it's amazing how many of them guests will eat. It is easy to change the flavor of a hard-cooked egg to mix and match with the other foods offered. Rather than add the standard Dijon mustard and Worcestershire, stir in finely chopped herbs, such as parsley or dill alone or along with some grated Parmesan cheese or a dash of hot sauce.

12 large eggs

Dijon mustard to taste

mayonnaise to taste

Worcestershire sauce to taste

1½ tsp salt

ground white pepper to taste

½ bunch fresh dill

1. Place the eggs in a saucepan, add water to cover, and bring to a boil. Cover the pan with a tight-fitting lid, turn off the heat, and let the eggs stand for 20 minutes.

2. Rinse the eggs under running cold water until cool enough to handle. Peel the eggs and rinse under cold water as quickly as possible.

3. Carefully cut the eggs in half lengthwise and remove the yolks to a bowl. Mash the yolks together with the mustard and mayonnaise, using enough for the desired flavor and creamy consistency. Season with the Worcestershire, salt, and pepper.

4. Scrape the yolk mixture into a pastry bag fitted with a medium star tip and pipe into the hollow in the egg whites to form a slight dome. Garnish each egg with a sprig of dill.

Stuffed Grape Leaves

*L*AMB IN the filling makes these grape leaves especially hearty, and the full complement of Middle Eastern spices gives them a heady aroma. Their rich, warm flavors make them a soothing addition to a fall or winter buffet.

1 cup minced onions

¼ cup finely diced green onions

2 Tbsp chopped parsley

1½ tsp minced garlic

4 Tbsp olive oil

3 large eggs, beaten

1 lb 8 oz ground lamb

1 cup cooked rice

½ cup pine nuts, toasted

2 Tbsp minced ginger

1 Tbsp chopped dill

1 Tbsp chopped mint

1½ tsp chopped oregano

1½ tsp ground turmeric

1½ tsp ground cumin

½ tsp ground cinnamon

1½ tsp fennel seeds

2 tsp salt

½ tsp ground black pepper

36 grape leaves, soaked in water

3 cups chicken stock, hot

BRUSHING SAUCE

¼ cup olive oil

1 Tbsp chopped mint

1½ tsp chopped oregano

3 Tbsp lemon juice

1. Sauté the onions, green onions, parsley, and garlic in the oil in a sauté pan until the onions are tender. Set aside to cool.

2. Combine the eggs, lamb, rice, pine nuts, ginger, herbs, spices, fennel seeds, salt, and pepper in a bowl and mix well. Add the cooled onion mixture and mix well.

3. Place 2 Tbsp of the filling in a grape leaf, fold in the ends of the leaf over the filling and roll up. Repeat with the remaining filling and grape leaves.

4. Place the finished grape leaves in a large saucepan, seam side down. Add enough stock to barely cover the leaves. Cover with a lid and bake in a preheated 350°F oven until the leaves are tender, about 1 hour.

5. Combine all ingredients for the sauce in a bowl and brush the mixture over the finished grape leaves.

Small Seared Lobster and Vegetable Quesadillas

SMOKED CHICKEN is a good substitute for the lobster. Its rich, smoky flavor completely changes the quesadilla but works well with the spices and buttery poblanos. Make it both ways for one event to add another item to the menu.

3 lb 8 oz lobster (about 2 whole)

½ tsp cumin seeds, toasted and ground

¼ tsp chili powder

pinch of cayenne

6 Tbsp olive oil or more if needed

½ cup finely diced onion

1½ tsp chopped garlic

7 oz poblanos, roasted and cut into ¼-in dice

3 oz red pepper, roasted and cut into ¼-in dice

pinch of salt

3 oz queso blanco, grated

8 flour tortillas (8-in diameter)

1. Cook the lobsters in simmering salted water for 6 minutes, shell, and place the meat in a bowl. Add the cumin, chili powder, and cayenne and toss to coat.

2. Heat 4 Tbsp oil in a sauté pan over high heat and pan-sear the lobster. Remove the lobster to a cutting board and cut into ¼-in dice.

3. Heat 2 Tbsp oil in the same (unwashed) sauté pan over medium heat and sauté the onion and garlic until soft, about 8 minutes, adding more oil if necessary to keep the mixture from sticking to the pan. Mix the onion, poblanos, and red pepper together and season with salt. Combine the lobster with the vegetable mixture and the queso blanco.

4. Using a 2½-in ring mold, cut 20 rounds from the tortillas for appetizer-size quesadillas.

5. Heat a little oil in a sauté pan and lightly sauté both sides of the tortilla rounds over medium-high heat. Place 1 Tbsp filling on each of 10 tortilla rounds and top with the remaining rounds.

6. Arrange the assembled quesadillas on a parchment-lined baking sheet. Place a half sheet of parchment paper on top of the quesadillas. Weigh down with another baking sheet to flatten.

7. Bake in a preheated 400°F oven until the cheese is melted, 8 to 10 minutes, or brown the quesadillas in a cast-iron pan. Serve immediately.

Pork Piccadillo Empanadas

MAKES 30 EMPANADAS

*T*HIS TRADITIONAL Spanish turnover is typically made in different shapes to identify different types of fillings. Try creating "house blend" fillings and shapes to add specialized variety to the family table.

PORK FILLING

2 tsp olive oil or vegetable oil

12 oz pork loin, coarsely ground

1 Tbsp minced jalapeño

2 tsp chili powder

1 tsp ground cumin

1 tsp ground cinnamon

¼ tsp ground allspice

¼ cup golden raisins, plumped in warm water

¼ cup blanched almonds, toasted and chopped

3½ Tbsp lime juice

1 tsp salt

½ tsp ground black pepper

2 Tbsp sour cream

EMPANADA DOUGH

1½ cups all-purpose flour

½ cup masa harina

3½ tsp baking powder

1 tsp salt

4 oz lard, melted and cooled

¾ cup water

2 large eggs

oil for deep frying

8 oz Salsa Verde (page 43), Salsa Fresca (page 41), or Chipotle Pico de Gallo (page 42)

AT LEFT: Empanadas, here shown being filled with pork, can also be filled with beef, lamb, or chicken to add variety to a buffet spread.

1. Heat the oil in a sauté pan over medium heat. Add the pork and sauté, breaking up the meat, until it is no longer pink, about 10 minutes. Stir in the jalapeño, chili powder, cumin, cinnamon, and allspice. Continue to sauté until most of the liquid evaporates, 5 to 6 minutes more. Transfer to a bowl and fold in the raisins and almonds. Season with the lime juice, salt, and pepper. Fold in the sour cream, adding just enough to gently bind the filling. Cool the filling, cover, and refrigerate until ready to assemble the empanadas, up to 2 days.

2. To prepare the dough, blend the flour, masa, baking powder, and salt in a mixing bowl. Add the lard and mix by hand or on low speed until evenly moistened. Blend ½ cup water and 1 egg and add the mixture gradually to the dough, stirring or blending with a dough hook as you work. Knead the dough until it is pliable, about 3 minutes.

3. Whisk together the remaining egg and ¼ cup water to make an egg wash.

4. To assemble the empanadas, roll out the dough very thin (¹⁄₁₆ in thick) and cut into 3-in rounds to make at least 30 rounds. Place 1 Tbsp filling on each round. Brush the edges with egg wash, fold in half, and seal the seams. Transfer to parchment-lined sheet pans, cover, and refrigerate until ready to fry.

5. Heat the oil in a deep fryer (or to a 2-in depth in a deep saucepan) to 350°F. Add empanadas to the hot oil and fry, turning if necessary to brown both sides evenly, until golden brown and crisp, 4 to 5 minutes. Drain and blot briefly with paper towels. Serve very hot with a salsa or pico de gallo.

STORAGE: The empanadas can be covered with plastic wrap and refrigerated for up to 24 hours, or frozen for up to 3 weeks.

Fried Wontons with Mustard Sauce

MAKES 20 WONTONS

Do not use too much filling or the wontons will be difficult to seal and may break open during frying or as guests try to eat them. It's better to have more perfect wontons than fewer overfilled ones.

MUSTARD SAUCE

¾ cup Dijon mustard

¼ cup water

1½ tsp sugar

1½ tsp soy sauce

1½ tsp vinegar

FILLING

4 oz ground pork

2 oz Chinese cabbage, thinly sliced

2 green onions, thinly sliced

1 tsp minced ginger

1 tsp soy sauce

1 tsp salt

¼ tsp ground black pepper

½ tsp dark sesame oil

1 large egg

2 Tbsp cold water

20 wonton skins

oil for deep frying

1. Combine the ingredients for the mustard sauce in a small bowl and mix well. Set aside.

2. Mix filling ingredients together in a medium bowl. Beat the egg with the water in a small bowl. To assemble the wontons, brush the edges of each wrapper with the egg wash. Place 2 teaspoons of the filling into each wrapper. Fold the wonton in half to make a triangle. Press to seal the edges securely. Bring the two corners along the base of the triangle in toward each other, overlap them, and press to seal securely. Transfer to a parchment-lined sheet pan and refrigerate until ready to fry.

3. Deep fry the wontons in a deep saucepan of hot oil until golden brown. Remove to a sheet pan lined with paper towels to drain.

4. Serve with the mustard sauce.

AT RIGHT: When making fried wontons, prepare and cook in small batches so that the dough doesn't dry out.

Steamed Wontons with Shrimp

MAKES 36 WONTONS

*M*AKE A sample wonton, steam it, and taste for seasoning. Make any necessary adjustments before filling the remaining wrappers.

½ lb shrimp, peeled and deveined

1 Tbsp dark sesame oil

1½ tsp sugar

1 Tbsp finely minced garlic

1 tsp finely minced ginger

1 Tbsp minced parsley

½ tsp salt

pinch of ground black pepper

⅔ cup uncooked brown rice, completely cooked
in 1⅓ cups of water

36 wonton wrappers

GARNISH

1 green onion, thinly sliced on the diagonal

2 Tbsp toasted sesame seeds

1. Make the filling by puréeing the shrimp, sesame oil, sugar, garlic, ginger, parsley, salt, and pepper into a coarse paste in a food processor, pulsing the machine on and off in short blasts. Transfer the shrimp mixture to a bowl. Purée the rice in the food processor very briefly, just enough to break up the grains. Fold the rice into the shrimp mixture until evenly blended.

2. To assemble the wontons, brush the edges of each wrapper with water (work with a few at a time so the wrappers will not dry out). Transfer the shrimp and rice filling to a pastry bag without a tip and pipe 1 tsp filling (about the size of a marble) onto the center of each wrapper. Fold the wonton in half to make a triangle. Press to seal the edges securely. Bring the two corners along the base of the triangle in toward each other, overlap them, and press to seal securely. Transfer to a parchment-lined sheet pan and refrigerate until ready to steam.

3. Cover the grate of a steamer with a single layer of lettuce leaves. Fill the bottom of the steamer, or the pan the steamer will rest in for cooking, with 1½ to 2 in of water. Place the steamer over the pan of water, place the lid on top, and preheat so that the water is just barely simmering.

4. Arrange the wontons over the surface of the lettuce leaves, making sure they do not touch. Replace the top and steam until the dough is firm to the touch, 5 to 10 minutes. Repeat with the remaining wontons.

NOTE: You can assemble these wontons ahead of time, and put them in an airtight container. They can be stored in the refrigerator for up to 24 hours or frozen for up to 3 weeks. If the wontons are frozen, steam them straight from the freezer and add a few minutes to the cooking time.

Smoked Salmon Tea Sandwiches

THE CHOPPED chives in this sandwich brighten the flavor of the salmon and complement the cool, creamy texture of the crème fraîche.

1 cup crème fraîche

2 Tbsp chopped chives

20 thin slices whole wheat bread

1 lb smoked salmon, thinly sliced

1. Combine the crème fraîche and chives in a bowl.

2. Spread each slice of bread with the crème fraîche mixture. Lay salmon slices over half of the bread slices and top with the remaining bread. Using a 1½-in-diameter cutter, cut 4 rounds from each sandwich.

CRÈME FRAÎCHE

Crème fraîche is made by fermenting heavy cream that has a butterfat content of about 60 percent with lactic acid and the appropriate bacteria cultures.

Newly prepared crème fraîche has a sweet flavor and loose, almost pourable texture. As it ages, its flavor becomes more tart and the consistency thickens to a point at which it can nearly hold a spoon upright.

To make your own crème fraîche, combine 32 fl oz of heavy cream with 8 oz buttermilk and let the mixture set, covered, at room temperature for 24 hours.

Smoked Salmon and Lemon-Herb Tea Sandwiches

MAKES 20 SANDWICHES

S MOKED FISH pair extremely well with the acidity of lemon and the refreshing flavors of herbs. Smoked white fish, such as trout or haddock, can be substituted for the salmon in this tea sandwich.

LEMON-HERB BUTTER

½ lb (2 sticks) unsalted butter, at room temperature

2 Tbsp sliced green onions

2 Tbsp chopped dill

5 Tbsp chopped parsley

1¼ tsp minced garlic

2 tsp lemon juice

1 tsp grated lemon zest

½ tsp kosher salt

¼ tsp freshly ground pepper

10 slices whole-grain bread

5 oz smoked salmon, thinly sliced

1. Place the softened butter in a bowl and beat using an electric mixer until smooth and creamy. Add the green onions, dill, parsley, and garlic and mix well. Season with the lemon juice and zest, salt, and pepper. Set aside.

3. Lay out the slices of bread on a work surface and spread the top side of each with a thin layer of herb butter, approximately 2 teaspoons. Place about 1 ounce of the smoked salmon on each of the slices, making sure to completely cover the bread. Top with the remaining bread slices, butter side down.

4. Wrap the sandwiches with plastic wrap and refrigerate until the butter is cold.

5. Transfer the sandwiches to a cutting board and cut off the crusts. Cut each large sandwich into 4 even squares.

Chive Cream Cheese and Cucumber Tea Sandwiches

ELEGANT IN their simplicity, these chive cream cheese and cucumber tea sandwiches are ideal for a summer cocktail party or any occasion where a light and refreshing hors d'oeuvre is welcome.

24 slices white bread

4 Tbsp chopped chives

6 oz cream cheese, at room temperature

1 English cucumber, sliced into thin rounds

3 Tbsp chopped dill

1. Using a 2-in round cookie cutter, cut out the center of the bread slices.

2. In a bowl, mix the chopped chives into the softened cream cheese.

3. Spread the chive cream cheese on one side of 12 bread rounds. Top with the cucumber slices, sprinkle with dill, and cover with the remaining bread rounds.

4. Cover with plastic wrap until ready to serve.

Roquefort Butter and Red Pear Tea Sandwiches

FOR A milder variation of this recipe, substitute the blue cheese with brie or goat's milk cheese, both of which pair extremely well with the red pears.

1 lemon, juiced

2 Tbsp water

1 red pear, cored and very thinly sliced

4 oz Roquefort, crumbled

½ cup (1 stick) unsalted butter, at room temperature

¼ tsp freshly ground pepper

16 thin slices white bread or brioche

1. Combine the lemon juice and water in a small bowl and add the pear slices. Keep the pear slices immersed until ready to use.

2. To make the sandwiches: Drain the pear slices and blot dry with paper towels.

3. Combine the Roquefort, butter, and pepper in a bowl and gently stir to mix, leaving small bits of cheese whole; do not overmix.

4. Lay out the slices of bread on the work surface. Spread the top side of each with a thin layer of Roquefort butter. Cover 8 slices with pears, overlapping slightly, and top each with a remaining bread slice, buttered side down.

5. Trim off the crusts using a serrated knife and cut each sandwich into three (1 × 3-in) rectangles.

6. Arrange the sandwiches on a platter and keep covered with damp paper towels until ready to serve.

Roast Beef and Stilton Tea Sandwiches

MAKES 20 SANDWICHES

STILTON IS Great Britain's historic blue cheese and complements another British favorite, roast beef. The Stilton can be replaced by a milder cheese such as brie or aged cheddar.

1 cup crumbled Stilton or other blue cheese

½ cup mayonnaise

1 Tbsp minced chives

1 Tbsp lemon juice

40 slices cocktail bread, 2½-inch square

½ bunch watercress, trimmed, leaves and tender stems only

1 lb sliced roast beef

¼ tsp freshly ground pepper

1. Combine the blue cheese, mayonnaise, chives, and lemon juice in a small bowl and stir gently to mix. Set aside.

2. Lay out the slices of bread on the work surface and spread the top side of each slice with a thin layer of the Stilton mixture. Top half of the slices with enough watercress leaves to completely cover the bread. (It is nice if some of the leaves extend just a little over the edge to give a nice contrast when presented.)

3. Top the watercress with one slice of the roast beef. Season lightly with pepper and close the sandwich with a second slice of bread. Serve immediately, or place the sandwiches in a container, cover tightly, and refrigerate until ready to serve.

Watercress and Olive Tea Sandwiches

MAKES 20 SANDWICHES

W ATERCRESS IS a spicy green that is balanced by the sweeter olives in this tea sandwich. Arugula can be substituted for the watercress, and for a different flavor combination garlic-stuffed olives are a delicious replacement for the pimiento-stuffed olives.

½ cup (1 stick) butter, at room temperature

8 oz cream cheese, softened

1 cup finely chopped watercress

⅓ cup pimiento-stuffed olives, finely chopped

10 slices (¼ in thick) from a Pullman loaf

1. Put the butter in a bowl and stir until light and fluffy. Add the cream cheese, watercress, and olives and stir until thoroughly mixed.

2. Lay out the slices of bread on the work surface and spread the top side of each with a thin layer of butter mixture. Spread the butter on each of 5 slices of bread.

3. Cover with the remaining slices, buttered side down, to make sandwiches.

4. Wrap the sandwiches in foil and refrigerate for a minimum of 30 minutes.

5. Trim the crusts and cut each sandwich into 4 individual rounds.

Shrimp Sandwiches

MAKES 20 SANDWICHES

A VARIATION ON the more traditional chicken or tuna salad, these shrimp sandwiches combine the classic ingredients for a shrimp cocktail into an hors d'oeuvre–size portion.

4 oz cream cheese, softened

2 Tbsp mayonnaise

1 Tbsp ketchup

1 tsp prepared mustard

¼ tsp garlic powder

1 cup chopped cooked shrimp

¼ cup finely chopped celery

1 tsp finely chopped onion

10 slices lightly buttered sandwich bread (buttered on one side only)

1. Combine the cream cheese, mayonnaise, ketchup, mustard, and garlic powder in a bowl and mix well. Stir in the shrimp, celery, and onion.

2. Lay out the bread slices, buttered side up, on the work surface and spread the top side of 5 slices of bread with the shrimp mixture. Cover with the other slices, buttered side down.

3. Trim the crusts and cut each sandwich into 4 even triangles.

4. Arrange the sandwiches on a platter and keep covered with plastic wrap until ready to serve.

Egg Salad Tea Sandwiches

SERVE THESE classic tea sandwiches at a luncheon buffet. Some crisp, fresh watercress makes a lovely accompaniment or garnish to layer in the sandwiches.

10 hard-cooked eggs, chopped

2 Tbsp chopped celery

2 Tbsp thinly sliced green onions

2 Tbsp cider vinegar

¾ cup mayonnaise

salt to taste

ground white pepper to taste

14 slices white bread, crusts removed

1. Combine the eggs, celery, green onions, vinegar, mayonnaise, salt, and pepper in a large bowl and mix well.

2. Spread the egg salad over half of the bread slices. Top each slice with the remaining bread and cut each sandwich crosswise in each direction to make 4 smaller square tea sandwiches.

HOW TO HARD-BOIL EGGS

A perfect hard-boiled egg should have firm, but tender whites and a fully coagulated yolk. Put the eggs carefully into a pot of either cold or simmering water. The water should be about 2 inches above the eggs.

Bring the water to a simmer, but do not let it boil rapidly. Boiling the eggs will make the whites touch and could cause the eggs to crack. Begin to time the cooking as soon as the water comes to a simmer. Hard-boiled eggs should simmer for 12 to 13 minutes.

The gray or green circle that often appears around the yolk of a hard-boiled egg is caused by a chemical reaction between iron and sulfur that is naturally found in eggs. To prevent this ring from forming, do not overcook the eggs and quickly cool them in cold water.

AT LEFT: Egg Salad Tea Sandwiches (back) and Smoked Salmon Tea Sandwiches (front, page 79)

Smoked Trout Canapé

MAKES 30 CANAPÉS

SMOKED TROUT has a wonderful buttery quality that is the perfect foil for the flavors of the horseradish and pimiento-stuffed olives. Use rye bread with caraway seeds for these canapés; the flavor of the caraway seeds is a delicious complement to the bread topping.

15 oz hot-smoked trout

30 rye bread canapé bases, toasted

1 cup plus 1 Tbsp Horseradish Butter (recipe follows), softened

10 pimiento-stuffed olives, sliced

1. Flake the trout into a bowl following natural seams into ¾- to 1-in-wide pieces.

2. To assemble the canapés: Spread each canapé base with 1 tsp Horseradish Butter; top with a piece of trout. Garnish with a slice of olive.

HORSERADISH BUTTER

MAKES 1 CUP

USE THIS flavored butter for spreading on bread to make grilled cheese sandwiches, it will lightly flavor the bread and complement the creamy cheese interior.

3 Tbsp prepared horseradish

1 cup (2 sticks) butter, softened

2 tsp prepared mustard

1 tsp Worcestershire sauce

1½ tsp sugar

½ tsp lemon juice

1. Squeeze excess liquid out of the horseradish. Combine all ingredients in a bowl and mix well.

2. Transfer the butter onto a piece of plastic wrap. Roll into a 1-in cylinder and secure ends by twisting. Store in the refrigerator until needed. Remove as much butter at a time as is needed for spreading and soften at room temperature.

Smoked Duck Mousse Canapé
with Raspberry

MAKES 30 CANAPÉS

*I*F RASPBERRIES are out of season, substitute apricot purée and dried apricots cut into quarters. For additional flavor, marinate the apricots in some dry sherry overnight.

4 oz smoked duck, diced

2 tsp powdered gelatin

2 Tbsp cold water

¼ cup heavy cream, whipped

2 Tbsp raspberry purée, strained (see Note)

½ cup (1 stick) butter, softened

30 (1½-in-diameter) round whole wheat canapé bases

30 thin slices smoked duck breast (cut to dimension of canapé base)

30 fresh raspberries

1. Purée the diced duck until smooth in a food processor.

2. Sprinkle the gelatin over the cold water in a small bowl and stir to break up any clumps. Let the gelatin soften in the water for about 3 minutes. Heat the softened gelatin over simmering water or in a microwave for about 20 seconds on low power until the granules melt and the mixture is clear. Add the gelatin to the duck and fold in the cream.

3. Blend the raspberry purée and butter in a bowl until smooth.

4. Spread the raspberry butter on each base. Pipe the mousse onto the canapé base; garnish with a slice of duck and a raspberry.

STORAGE: The mousse is best if prepared as close as possible to serving time. When preparing these canapés, prepare the raspberry purée first and have all other ingredients and tools ready.

NOTE: To prepare a raspberry purée, purée berries in a blender or food processor. Strain through a fine sieve. Taste and adjust seasoning as required with sugar and a few drops of balsamic vinegar.

Prosciutto and Melon Canapé

MAKES 30 CANAPÉS

*T*O PREPARE the mascarpone cheese spread, add Tabasco, Dijon mustard, salt, and pepper to 1 cup of mascarpone and mix well. Use only a small amount of the Tabasco and mustard to preserve the delicate flavor of the mascarpone.

8 very thin slices prosciutto (about 5 oz)

30 (1½-in-diameter) round white bread canapé bases, toasted

5 oz mascarpone cheese spread

45 pieces honeydew melon, scooped into small balls

45 pieces cantaloupe, cut into small dice

GARNISH

30 mint leaves

1. Cut the prosciutto to fit the canapé bases.

2. To assemble the canapés, spread the canapé bases with some of the mascarpone spread and top with a piece of prosciutto. Pipe a small mound of mascarpone in the center of each canapé and top with 3 melon balls. Top each canapé with a mint leaf.

Goat's Milk Cheese Canapés with Sweet Peppers

MAKES 30 CANAPÉS

THIS CHEESE-AND-PEPPER combination also works well with queso blanco, a traditional Mexican cheese, which blends well with the flavors of the jalapeño and cilantro. Queso blanco is made from cow's milk and has a slightly sweeter flavor than does goat's milk cheese.

½ jalapeño, seeded and minced

15 oz Roasted Pepper Salad (page 135)

8 oz soft fresh goat's milk cheese

8½ oz clabbered cream or sour cream

30 (1½-in diameter) round whole wheat bread canapé bases, toasted

30 cilantro leaves, loosely packed

1. Add the jalapeño to the pepper salad and marinate for at least 30 minutes.

2. Blend the goat's milk cheese and clabbered cream in a bowl until smooth and pipeable.

3. Using a pastry bag fitted with a medium-sized star tip, pipe the cheese mixture in a ring around the canapé base. Mound about 1 Tbsp of the pepper salad in the center and top with a cilantro leaf.

GOAT'S MILK CHEESE

Goat's milk cheese, or chèvre, is a fresh or ripened cheese with a smooth, creamy texture and a slightly acidic finish. Goat's milk cheeses are often found coated in a layer of food-grade ash, which helps to both age the cheese and mellow its acidity. Its tanginess is complimented by many ingredients including herbs, olives, hot and sweet peppers, and spices. Goat's milk cheese can be purchased with these flavors already mixed into the cheese.

Figs and goat's milk cheese is a classic pairing which makes an elegant canapé when served with a port wine reduction on a disc of short dough (see Rich Short Dough, page 183).

For a simple and fast hors d'ouevre, serve various flavored goat's milk cheeses with an assortment of crackers and savory jellies or chutneys. Goat's milk cheese on a garlic crostini is also delicious and easy to prepare.

Asparagus and Prosciutto Open-Face Tea Sandwiches

MAKES 20 SERVINGS

T HE PINK prosciutto against the green asparagus makes these hors d'oeuvre an attractive presentation. This is a modern twist on the classic luncheon tea sandwich.

40 spears asparagus

6 thin slices prosciutto di Parma

2 Tbsp Dijon mustard

10 slices bread (¼ in thick) from a Pullman loaf

½ cup cream cheese, softened and whipped

¼ tsp freshly ground pepper

1. Trim the ends of the asparagus. If you want to use the asparagus stems in another dish, peel the stem, starting about 1 inch below the tip. Bring a large pot of salted water to a rolling boil. Fill a large bowl with ice water (to cool the asparagus after it cooks).

2. Add the asparagus to the boiling water and cook until the stems are tender to the bite; the tips should still hold together, about 4 minutes. Immediately drain the asparagus and cool by submerging in ice water. Once cool, lift the asparagus from the water, drain well, and blot dry. Trim off the tips to use in the finger sandwiches. Reserve the stems for another use.

3. Trim the prosciutto slices carefully to remove excess fat. Cut the lean portion of the prosciutto into small strips, each about ½ inch wide and 2 or 3 inches long. Spread the strips with a small amount of the mustard and wrap one asparagus tip in each strip as follows: Hold one end of the strip just below the tip and wrap the prosciutto around the asparagus, overlapping it slightly as you wrap, to completely cover all but the tip. Continue until all of the asparagus is wrapped.

4. Trim the crusts from the bread and spread the slices evenly with the cream cheese. Season with black pepper. Lay two wrapped asparagus spears on each slice of bread. Cut each slice of bread in half, creating two sandwiches. Serve immediately, or place the sandwiches in a container, cover tightly, and refrigerate until ready to serve.

Cucumber and Mint Tea Sandwiches

MAKES 24 SANDWICHES

THE CRISP cucumber and the brightly flavored mint make these refreshing tea sandwiches an ideal hors d'oeuvre choice for a spring or summer party.

6 Tbsp butter, whipped

2 Tbsp fresh mint leaves, chopped

1 tsp salt

½ tsp freshly ground pepper

12 thin slices white sandwich bread, crust removed

1 cucumber, peeled and thinly sliced

1. Stir the butter and mint in a small bowl until mixed. Stir in ½ tsp salt and ¼ tsp pepper.

2. Lay out the slices of bread on the work surface and spread the top side of each with a thin layer of butter mixture, about 1½ teaspoons.

3. Lay the cucumber on 6 slices of the bread and sprinkle with the remaining salt and pepper.

4. Cover with the remaining 6 slices of bread and cut each sandwich into 4 squares.

5. Arrange the sandwiches on a platter and keep covered with plastic wrap until ready to serve.

Dilled Salmon Cream Cheese Tea Sandwiches

MAKES 40 SANDWICHES

SMOKED SALMON, fresh dill, and cream cheese are a classic combination for good reason. The textures and flavors complement each other perfectly and when the ingredients are rolled up in a thin slice of pumpernickel bread, these hors d'oeuvre are as easy to eat as they are to make.

8 oz low-fat cream cheese, softened

1 Tbsp chopped dill

1 Tbsp chopped green onions

½ tsp hot pepper sauce

½ tsp salt

¼ tsp freshly ground pepper

10 slices pumpernickel bread

5 oz smoked salmon

1. Combine the cream cheese, dill, green onions, pepper sauce, salt, and pepper in a bowl.

2. Trim the crusts from the slices of bread with a sharp or serrated knife.

3. Flatten each slice of bread using a rolling pin.

4. Lay out the slices of bread on the work surface and spread the top side of each with 1 Tbsp of the cream cheese mixture.

5. Cover the cream cheese completely with the smoked salmon.

6. Roll up each slice of bread with the salmon and cream cheese.

7. Cut each roll crosswise into 4 pinwheels.

8. Arrange each of the rounds on a platter and keep covered with plastic wrap until ready to serve.

Goat's Milk Cheese and Roasted Pepper Crostini

MAKES 34 CROSTINI

THE TANGY goat's milk cheese pairs particularly well with the slightly sweet roasted peppers in this simple, yet sophisticated crostini. Try replacing the basil in this recipe with chopped capers for a more full-bodied winter hors d'oeuvre.

1 red pepper

1 yellow pepper

1 green pepper

1 cup olive oil

1 tsp salt

½ tsp freshly ground pepper

1 baguette

3 garlic cloves, peeled and cut in half

1 (12-oz) log goat's milk cheese

1 Tbsp chopped thyme

2 Tbsp basil, cut into chiffonade

1. Preheat the oven to 400°F. Cut the peppers in half; remove and discard the seeds and ribs. Rub lightly with oil and place cut side down on a baking sheet. Roast until the skin blisters and darkens, about 20 minutes. Remove from the oven, cover tightly with foil or a second baking sheet turned upside down over the peppers. Steam until they are cool enough to handle (at least 1 hour). Pull away the skin and discard (use a paring knife to help with any pieces that don't come away easily). Cut into fine, short julienne, transfer to a container, and add ⅔ cup olive oil, the salt, and ¼ tsp pepper. Stir to coat the peppers evenly. Cover and marinate in the refrigerator for at least 3 or up to 8 hours before using.

2. Preheat the oven to 325°F. Brush the baguette slices lightly with oil on both sides, place on a baking sheet, and bake until the crostini are dry and lightly toasted (a light golden brown), about 15 minutes. While the crostini are still hot, pierce half of a garlic clove with a fork and rub the crostini with the garlic, replacing the piece of garlic as it is used up. (This can be done a day ahead of time.)

3. Brush the goat's milk cheese log with the oil and roll in a mixture of the chopped thyme leaves and the remaining ¼ tsp black pepper. Slice thinly. Top each crostini with a slice of the goat's milk cheese and 1 teaspoon of the roasted peppers. Scatter the basil chiffonade over the crostini and serve.

Herbes de Provence Tea Sandwiches

HERBES DE Provence is a combination of rosemary, marjoram, basil, savory, thyme, and sometimes lavender. These aromatic herbs give a boost of flavor to the fresh tomatoes in this tea sandwich.

4 oz cream cheese, whipped

1 Tbsp herbes de Provence

12 thin slices white sandwich bread

5 tomatoes, peeled, seeded, chopped, and patted dry with paper towels

1 tsp sea salt

¼ tsp freshly ground pepper

1. Combine the cream cheese and herbes de Provence in a bowl using a mixer and mix until smooth, about 2 minutes.

2. Spread about 2 tsp of the cream cheese mixture onto each slice of bread.

3. Cover half of the slices with the tomatoes, and sprinkle with the salt and pepper.

4. Cover with the remaining slices of bread.

5. Cut each sandwich into 4 rectangles. Wrap in plastic wrap until ready to serve.

Radish Poppy-Seed Tea Sandwiches

*T*HE HOT radishes are mellowed slightly by the cream cheese in this tea sandwich. Both the crisp radishes and the poppy seeds contribute an appealing crunch.

4 oz cream cheese, softened

½ cup minced radishes

1 tsp poppy seeds

¼ tsp salt

¼ tsp freshly ground pepper

8 slices rye bread

¼ cup (½ stick) unsalted butter, at room temperature

12 leaves arugula, spinach, or radicchio

1. Combine the cream cheese, radishes, poppy seeds, salt, and pepper in a bowl and mix well.

2. Lay out the bread slices on the work surface and spread the top side of each with a thin layer of butter.

3. Spread half of the cream cheese mixture onto the buttered side of 2 pieces of bread.

4. Top with arugula, spinach, or radicchio and place the remaining slices of bread, buttered side down, on top of the cream cheese mixture.

5. Cut the crusts off the sandwiches and cut each sandwich into 4 triangles. Wrap in plastic wrap until ready to serve.

Potato Crêpes with Crème Fraîche and Caviar

MAKES 30 PIECES

FOR ADDITIONAL flavor, add fresh dill to the crêpe batter. Chop a tablespoon or two of fresh dill. Warm the heavy cream for the crêpes in a small saucepan, remove it from the heat, and add the fresh dill. Let the cream cool completely before using it to prepare the crêpe batter.

12 oz puréed cooked potatoes

¼ cup all-purpose flour

2 large eggs

3 large egg whites

¼ cup heavy cream or as needed

salt to taste

ground white pepper to taste

pinch of grated nutmeg

6 oz smoked salmon slices

½ cup crème fraîche

1 oz caviar

1. Combine the potatoes and flour in a mixer. Add the eggs one at a time, and then mix in the whites. Adjust the consistency with cream to that of a pancake batter; season with the salt, pepper, and nutmeg.

2. Coat a nonstick griddle or sauté pan lightly with oil. Pour the batter as for pancakes into silver-dollar-size portions. Cook until golden brown and turn and finish on the second side, about 2 minutes total cooking time.

3. Serve the crêpes warm, each topped with a smoked salmon slice and garnished with a small dollop of crème fraîche and caviar.

AT LEFT: Hors d'oeuvre that are easy to assemble, such as these Potato Crêpes with Crème Fraîche and Caviar, can be easily converted from a passed item to a showpiece on a buffet table on which the components are laid out and guests assemble each serving on their own.

Sushi

MAKES 24 PIECES

L ET THE rice cool completely before spreading it on the nori sheets. The heat will bring out a briny flavor and pungent aroma in the seaweed and will overwhelm the other flavors in the sushi.

½ cup short-grain rice

2 Tbsp rice vinegar plus as needed

2¼ tsp sugar

2 tsp salt

3 sheets nori

½ cup julienned avocado

½ cup julienned cucumber

½ cup crabmeat

1. Wash the rice 3 times or until the water runs clear. Add water so it comes 1 in over the rice and simmer until tender, about 20 minutes.

2. Warm 2 Tbsp vinegar with the sugar and salt in a saucepan, but do not boil.

3. Fold the warm vinegar mixture into the hot rice. Cool the rice completely.

4. Place a bamboo sushi-rolling mat on a cutting board and put 1 sheet of nori on top. Evenly spread one-third of the rice over the nori sheet, leaving a ½-in band along one of the long sides of the nori sheet exposed.

5. Place one-third of the avocado, cucumber, and crabmeat on the rice across the long edge of the nori sheet. Roll up carefully, brush the exposed strip of nori with rice vinegar, and press to seal. Repeat with the remaining nori, rice, avocado, cucumber, and crabmeat.

6. Cut each roll crosswise into 8 even pieces. Serve with pickled ginger and wasabi paste mixed with soy sauce.

VARIATIONS

CUCUMBER ROLL: Follow the recipe as stated above but sprinkle 1 tsp unhulled sesame seeds on the spread rice and replace the filling ingredients with 2 Tbsp julienned cucumber per roll.

AVOCADO ROLL: Follow the recipe as stated above but sprinkle 1 tsp unhulled sesame seeds on the spread rice and replace the filling ingredients with 2 Tbsp julienned avocado per roll.

AT RIGHT: Roll the sushi tightly so that it does not unravel when cut into portions or picked up.

Chapter Five

SKEWERED AND DIPPED

A GIFT FROM CAVE-DWELLER cooks, skewers are an essential element to any hors d'oeuvre party. Not only are they utensils for picking up bite-size portions of ready-to-eat foods (cheese, sausages, meatballs, cocktail shrimp), but they also hold raw foods, such as meats, seafood, or vegetables, while they cook, and keep them secure until they become hot hors d'oeuvre. Skewers make foods that are thought of as unruly or too cumbersome to serve as hors d'oeuvre (marinated roasted peppers, olives, dumplings) completely user-friendly.

Hors d'oeuvre can be cooked and served from the cooking skewer or bite-size chunks of cooked or ready-to-eat foods can be skewered just before arranging them on a serving platter. Skewers can eliminate the hassle and cleanup of plates, knives, and forks—just place an attractive bowl or container filled with skewers on the hors d'oeuvre table and tuck stacks of cocktail napkins and small, deep baskets lined with plastic bags around the room for not-so-subtle clues of trash-disposal sites. An appointed guardian can replace the liner bags before they overflow in vigilant, frequent turns as the food on the table is refreshed.

TYPES OF SKEWERS

There are three basic types of skewers: metal, wood, and bamboo. Metal skewers can be used again and again, but this is not a concern at an hors d'oeuvre party. What host wants their guests to worry about where to leave their metal skewers? In a Seinfeld-like way, it could affect the atmosphere of the party! Disposable skewers are the way to go.

Wood or bamboo skewers come in a variety of lengths or can be snipped to the exact size needed for the hors d'oeuvre on the menu. There are two drawbacks to wood or bamboo skewers: They must be soaked thoroughly before use in cooking or they will burn; and they are round, unlike metal skewers, which are usually squared, so the impaled foods don't spin on them while cooking. This is more of a concern with big chunks of food than it is with bite-size portions.

FOODS TO SKEWER AND SKEWERED COOKING METHODS

Vegetables, meats, poultry, and seafood are all fine choices of foods to cook on a skewer for hors d'oeuvre. The important thing to remember with them all is that they must be cut into a uniform size for even cooking. If you have large and small pieces on one skewer, the small pieces will be done when the large ones are still raw, and when the large ones are done the small ones will be hopelessly overcooked.

Cut vegetables into hors d'oeuvre–size chunks for spearing—potatoes, winter squashes, zucchini, and onions work best. Meats and poultry can be cut either into bite-size chunks or into thinner slices and threaded or woven onto the skewer. Seafood, such as shrimp, will not twirl on a skewer when it is threaded tail-to-head rather than through the body, and scallops stay put when skewered through the sides. The same skewer logic applies to small chunks of fish, which should be put onto the skewer perpendicular to the grain instead of with it.

Skewered hors d'oeuvre are typically marinated or brushed before cooking with barbecue or other sauce; are grilled, roasted, or broiled; and devoured without removing them from the skewers. The cooking time will be reduced if the ingredients are bite-size and they are not packed tightly onto the skewers.

PAIRING SKEWERS AND DIPS

Flavor combinations can be tricky. If you are a novice, it is good to stick to the basics. Use combinations that you know and are comfortable with before you get too adventurous with your guests. Typically, if you think of complementing or contrasting flavors, you will do well. Some examples of complementing flavors are sweet and rich or smoky and hot. Sweet and sour or hot with cool and mellow will contrast and balance each other.

ALMOST HOMEMADE

Store-Bought Marinades and Sauces

Foods that are cooked on a skewer are often marinated first and often basted with that marinade and served with a dipping sauce. There are many jarred marinades and sauces available—a favorite jarred salad dressing can be used. Taste the products before using them as they vary widely in flavor and quality. It's worth finding and stocking a selection of flavors of jarred marinades and sauces, as they are time-savers in a crunch.

Lamb Brochettes with Mint Pesto (page 111)

Chicken Saté with Peanut Sauce

MAKES 40 SATÉS

*T*HE PEANUT sauce is delicious served with tempura or tossed with some buckwheat soba noodles. Cilantro brightens the rich dense flavor of the peanuts, so add plenty.

2½ lb chicken thigh meat

MARINADE

1 cup peanut oil

½ stalk lemongrass, shredded

6 garlic cloves, minced

2½ Tbsp curry powder

1½ Tbsp honey

1½ tsp fish sauce

½ tsp red pepper flakes

PEANUT SAUCE

1 cup peanut butter

½ cup water

¼ cup lime juice

¼ cup soy sauce

2 Tbsp minced jalapeño with seeds

1 Tbsp minced garlic

1 Tbsp sugar

1 Tbsp peanut oil

1 tsp cayenne

¼ cup chopped cilantro plus extra leaves for garnish, if desired

1. Slice the chicken into finger-size pieces.

2. Combine the marinade ingredients in a bowl and mix well. Add the chicken and toss to coat. Cover with plastic wrap and marinate in the refrigerator 4 to 8 hours.

3. Soak forty 6-in bamboo skewers in water for 30 minutes to prevent burning.

4. To make the peanut sauce, combine all the ingredients in a saucepan and bring to a slow boil, stirring until smooth. Simmer until the sauce is the desired dipping consistency and adjust seasoning. Set aside.

5. Skewer the meat and grill until cooked through.

6. Serve the skewers with the peanut sauce. If desired, garnish the sauce with cilantro.

VARIATION

BEEF SATÉ: Replace the chicken with 2½ lb of top round trim and cut as for chicken.

AT RIGHT: Chicken Saté with Peanut Sauce

Chinese Skewered Bites

MAKES 30 SKEWERS

*T*HE PLUM sauce in the recipe gives this hors d'oeuvre a rich, full-bodied flavor. If you desire, you can use chicken, beef, or lamb instead of the pork.

1 qt dry red wine

3 cups minced green onions

¼ cup soy sauce

1 cup plum sauce

½ cup dark sesame oil

¼ cup sesame seeds, toasted

2 garlic cloves, finely minced

1 tsp dried thyme leaves

1 lb boneless pork loin, cut into bite-size pieces

1. Combine the wine, green onions, soy sauce, plum sauce, sesame oil, sesame seeds, garlic, and thyme in a small saucepan and boil for 5 minutes. Cool the mixture to room temperature. Put the pork in a shallow bowl and pour the marinade over the pork. Cover and refrigerate at least 1 hour.

2. Soak thirty 6-in bamboo skewers in water for 30 minutes to prevent burning. Remove the pork from the marinade and thread onto the skewers.

3. Pour the marinade into a saucepan and heat to boiling. Simmer the marinade until thickened to the desired consistency for dipping, about 10 minutes.

4. While the marinade simmers, broil or grill the meat until cooked through, 5 to 7 minutes.

5. Strain the marinade and use it for a dipping sauce for the pork.

Barbecued Shrimp and Bacon

MAKES 30 SKEWERS

*T*HESE SKEWERS are quick and easy to prepare. The Apricot-Ancho Sauce complements the smokiness of the bacon, but if you don't have the time to make it, a store-bought variety with a similar flavor mix will work well.

30 shrimp, peeled and deveined

15 strips smoked bacon, partially cooked and cut in half

1 cup Apricot-Ancho Barbecue Sauce (recipe follows)

1. Soak thirty 6-in bamboo skewers in water for 30 minutes to prevent burning. Wrap each shrimp with a bacon strip. Thread each shrimp on a bamboo skewer.

2. Place the skewers on a wire rack set into a foil-lined baking pan.

3. Broil the shrimp 1 to 2 minutes on the first side. Turn and broil until the bacon gets crisp and the shrimp are just cooked through, 1 to 2 minutes. Remove from the broiler and baste with the barbecue sauce.

APRICOT-ANCHO BARBECUE SAUCE

MAKES 4 CUPS

6 strips bacon, chopped

1½ cups small-dice yellow onion

1 tbsp minced garlic

¾ cup ketchup

¾ cup orange juice

¾ cup packed dark brown sugar

⅓ cup chopped dried apricots

¼ cup malt vinegar

2 anchos, diced

1 tsp dry mustard

1 tsp Tabasco sauce

1 tsp cayenne

2 tsp salt

1 tsp ground black pepper

1. Sauté the bacon in a large sauté pan over medium heat until almost crisp, about 4 minutes. Add the onions and sauté until browned, about 5 minutes. Add the garlic and sauté until aromatic, about 1 minute.

2. Add all the remaining ingredients. Simmer until the apricots are very soft, about 10 minutes. Taste the sauce and season with additional salt and pepper, if needed.

3. Transfer to a blender and purée until relatively smooth. The sauce is ready to use now, or it can be cooled and stored in a covered container in the refrigerator for up to 1 week.

Lamb Brochettes
with Mint Pesto

MAKES 30 BROCHETTES

THE CLASSIC combination of lamb and mint makes this hors d'oeuvre a favorite. If using bacon rather than pancetta, blanch it in a large saucepan of slowly simmering water for 5 minutes. The bacon will become opaque and firm. Drain and pat dry before using.

2 lb 8 oz boneless leg of lamb

2 Tbsp lemon juice (about ½ lemon)

3 large garlic cloves, crushed

1 tsp salt

½ tsp ground black pepper

¼ cup extra-virgin olive oil

2 Tbsp chopped mint, chopped

8 oz pancetta, thinly sliced, or bacon
    (about 15 slices)

2 cups mint pesto sauce (jarred or homemade)

1. Cut the lamb into ¾-in cubes. Combine the lemon juice, garlic, salt, and pepper in a large bowl and whisk until blended. Add the oil and mint.

2. Toss the lamb in the mixture to coat well, cover, and marinate in the refrigerator, tossing occasionally, at least 4 hours.

3. Soak thirty 6-in bamboo skewers in water for 30 minutes to prevent burning. Thread 2 pieces of lamb and ½ slice of pancetta onto each skewer; arrange on a sheet pan.

4. Roast the brochettes in a preheated 450°F oven until the lamb is nicely browned outside, yet still pink and juicy inside, 8 to 12 minutes.

5. Serve the brochettes with mint pesto sauce for dipping.

AT LEFT: When preparing skewered hors d'oeuvre, such as these miniature lamb brochettes, it is essential to soak the skewers in water for at least 30 minutes so that they don't burn during cooking.

Wrapped Shrimp with Asian Barbecue Sauce

MAKES 30 SKEWERS

*T*HE PINEAPPLE and coconut add a definite Southeast Asian flavor to this recipe. The coconut also adds a wonderful crunch and makes the skewers look even more enticing.

1 lb fresh trimmed pineapple

30 medium shrimp, peeled and deveined

1 tsp salt

¼ tsp ground black pepper

15 bacon slices, partially cooked and cut in half

1 Tbsp olive oil

1 cup diced onions

½ cup diced celery

1 garlic clove, chopped

½ cup ketchup

½ cup chili sauce

¼ cup plum sauce

2 Tbsp rice vinegar

2 Tbsp soy sauce

2 tsp Worcestershire sauce

1 cup thinly sliced green onions

¼ cup toasted coconut

1. Soak thirty 6-in bamboo skewers in water to prevent burning. Cut thirty ½-in chunks of pineapple and finely chop whatever remains.

2. Season the shrimp with salt and pepper. Place a chunk of pineapple on each shrimp and wrap with a piece of bacon.

3. Place a 6-in skewer through each shrimp unit and reserve. (Do not hold for too long or the pineapple will denature the shrimp.)

4. Heat the oil in a large skillet over medium heat and sweat the onions, celery, and garlic until softened but not brown, 3 to 4 minutes.

5. Add the reserved chopped pineapple, ketchup, chili sauce, plum sauce, vinegar, soy sauce, and Worcestershire sauce to the onion mixture. Bring to a simmer and cook until the sauce is glossy and thickened, 15 minutes. Adjust the consistency with water, if necessary, and season with salt and pepper. Keep the sauce warm.

6. To cook the shrimp, spoon or brush a small amount of sauce (about 1 tsp each) over each skewer and place in a preheated 400°F oven until the meat just turns white, about 10 minutes.

7. Remove the skewers from oven and neatly arrange on serving platters. Sprinkle with the green onions and coconut. Serve immediately with the remaining sauce on the side for dipping.

AT LEFT: Wrapped Shrimp with Asian Barbeque Sauce

Crab Cakes with Creole Honey-Mustard Sauce

MAKES 30 CRAB CAKES

THE JAPANESE-STYLE bread crumbs called panko make an extra-crispy exterior on these cakes. Serve them with honey mustard as suggested, or with conventional tartar sauce, an equally tasty option.

1 lb lump crabmeat, picked clean

2 bacon slices, cooked crisp and crumbled

2 green onions, minced

2 garlic cloves, minced

1 cup fresh white bread crumbs

¼ cup finely diced celery

2 tsp Dijon mustard

2 tsp dry mustard

1 tsp salt

pinch of cayenne

mayonnaise as needed

2 Tbsp lemon juice

1½ cups Japanese-style bread crumbs (panko)

1 cup vegetable oil

1 cup Creole honey-mustard sauce

1. Combine the crabmeat, bacon, green onions, garlic, white bread crumbs, celery, Dijon mustard, dry mustard, salt, cayenne, and mayonnaise in a large bowl and mix gently until blended, adding just enough mayonnaise to hold the mixture together. Blend in the lemon juice.

2. Portion the crab cakes into 30 balls, flatten slightly, and bread with the Japanese-style bread crumbs. (At this point, the cakes can be wrapped and refrigerated or frozen for later use.)

3. Heat the oil to 350°F in a sauté pan over medium heat. Pan fry the crab cakes in oil until heated through and golden brown on each side, about 4 minutes in all. Drain briefly on paper towels. Serve immediately with the honey-mustard sauce.

AT RIGHT: Crab Cakes with Creole Honey-Mustard Sauce

Shrimp Tempura

MAKES 30 PIECES

TEMPURA TAKES patience to fry perfectly and not turn out soggy. If too much food is added to the hot oil at once, it will drastically reduce the temperature, or "shock" it—and cause the coating batter to absorb oil.

3 cups all-purpose flour

5 tsp baking powder

½ tsp salt plus 1 Tbsp for sprinkling on the shrimp

3 cups cold water plus more if needed

¼ cup sesame oil

30 shrimp (26/30 count), peeled and deveined, tails left intact

½ tsp ground black pepper

1 qt vegetable oil, for deep frying

2 cups Tempura Dipping Sauce (recipe follows) or more if needed

1. Whisk together the flour, baking powder, and ½ tsp salt in a large bowl. Add the water and sesame oil all at once in a thin, steady stream while whisking and gently whisk until combined. (The batter should be very smooth and about the thickness of pancake batter.) Cover the bowl with plastic wrap and refrigerate the batter until ready to prepare the tempura.

2. Blot the shrimp dry with paper towels, season with 1 Tbsp salt and the pepper, and dip in the batter; hold the shrimp over the bowl, letting excess batter drip off.

3. Preheat the oil to 350°F in a large, deep saucepan or wok and deep fry the shrimp, in batches, until the tails turn a light pink color and the batter is puffed and light golden brown, 4 to 5 minutes per batch. Drain the shrimp on a sheet pan lined with paper towels. Keep the cooked shrimp warm in a low oven until the frying is complete.

4. Serve the shrimp immediately with the dipping sauce.

VARIATION

VEGETABLE TEMPURA: Substitute 2 lb 12 oz assorted vegetables (e.g., broccoli, zucchini, mushrooms) for the shrimp. Blot the vegetables dry before seasoning and frying them.

TEMPURA DIPPING SAUCE

MAKES 4 CUPS

2½ cups water

1¼ cups soy sauce

2 Tbsp minced ginger

6 Tbsp mirin (sweet rice wine)

3 Tbsp bonito flakes

Combine all ingredients in a bowl. Let the flavors blend for at least 1 hour at room temperature before serving.

AT RIGHT: When deep frying, cut foods into equal-sized pieces so that everything in a batch finishes cooking at the same time.

Petite Cod Cakes with
Black Olive Butter Sauce

MAKES 30 CAKES

THE FLAVORS of the sauce and garnish enhance the delicate flavor of the cod. Have small plates handy so your guests can get plenty of the sauce on each cake.

COD CAKES

1 lb potatoes, steamed or boiled and puréed (nothing added)

1 lb cod fillet, poached

2 Tbsp olive oil plus extra for sautéing

1 tsp minced garlic

½ tsp salt

pinch of cayenne

⅔ cup Black Olive Butter Sauce (recipe follows)

GARNISH

1 tomato, peeled, seeded, and cut into matchstick-size strips

¼ cup Niçoise olive slivers

¼ cup basil chiffonade

1. Combine the cod cake ingredients in a bowl, making sure to dry both the cod and the potatoes thoroughly before they are combined. Shape into thirty 1-in-diameter cylinders that are about 2 in tall.

2. Heat the olive oil in a large sauté pan and sauté the cakes, browning only on the tops and bottoms. Finish cooking the cakes on a sheet pan in a preheated 400°F oven for about 5 minutes.

3. To serve, toss the tomatoes, olives, and basil together in a bowl and sprinkle a bit on top of each cake. Serve the butter sauce on the side.

BLACK OLIVE BUTTER SAUCE

MAKES ABOUT ⅔ CUP

¼ cup red wine

1 sprig thyme

1 bay leaf

1 Tbsp minced shallots

2 Tbsp chopped Niçoise olives

2 Tbsp heavy cream

10 Tbsp (1¼ sticks) butter, soft

2 tsp soy sauce

salt to taste

ground black pepper to taste

1. Combine the wine, thyme, bay leaf, shallots, and olives in a small saucepan and simmer until reduced to a syrupy consistency.

2. Add the cream and reduce to coating consistency. Finish by whisking or swirling in the butter.

3. Season the sauce with the soy sauce, salt, and pepper; strain through a sieve.

Grilled Cinnamon Chicken Skewers

MAKES 36 PIECES

CINNAMON STICKS stand in for bamboo or metal skewers and infuse the chicken cubes with their distinctive flavor. This dish is easy to put together and gives an eye-catching presentation.

6 boneless, skinless chicken breasts, about 3 pounds

Cinnamon sticks, split in half lengthwise

¼ cup prepared plum sauce

¼ cup dry sherry

1 tablespoon hoisin sauce

1 tablespoon soy sauce

3 green onions, thinly sliced on the diagonal

2 tablespoons sesame seeds

1. Cut the chicken breasts into 2-inch cubes. Make a hole in the center of each cube and thread onto a cinnamon stick.

2. Mix together the plum sauce, sherry, hoisin sauce, and soy sauce. Toss the skewered chicken cubes to coat.

3. Preheat the grill to medium-high. Grill the chicken about 5 to 10 minutes. Transfer the chicken to a serving platter and sprinkle with the green onion and sesame seeds before serving.

Chapter Six

BOWLS AND PLATTERS

❦

FTER ITS FLAVOR, perhaps a food's presentation makes it a hit; the arrangement of the food on the platter will determine its appeal to guests. The colors, textures, and shapes of the bowls and platters can enhance the appearance of the hors d'oeuvre and reinforce the overall party theme at the same time. The colors of the foods displayed will determine the colors of the serving pieces to use. Plain, white china is always a safe choice to make when the menu contains foods in a myriad of colors, shapes, and sizes. Contrasting elements, such as a bright-colored dipping sauce next to an array of brochettes, stand out on white platters and will encourage guests' attention to the food. Balance eye-catching arrangements with a tray of canapés arranged in strong, clean lines so no one item stands out. A grouping of dishes, such as a selection of antipasti, could include a focal point, an obvious visual snare, which draws the eye to the buffet—a basket of tall, homemade grissini would do the trick.

GARNISHING FOODS SERVED IN BOWLS AND ON PLATTERS

When it comes to selecting hors d'oeuvre, guests generally choose those with a garnish over those without a clever bit of added color, flavor, or texture. There are many options to choose from when selecting an appropriate garnish. When serving hors d'oeuvre on a platter, garnish the platter rather than each hors d'oeuvre. In some cases, however, it will be more appealing or even necessary to the recipe to garnish each item on the platter.

EASY TERRINES AND PÂTÉS

Some of the more formal and elegant hors d'oeuvre are terrines and pâtés. Terrine is a shortened name for a dish classically known as pâté en terrine, and often in modern times terrines are referred to as pâtés. Terrines are forcemeat mixtures that have been baked in an earthenware mold with a tight-fitting lid.

A forcemeat is a lean meat and fat emulsion created by grinding, sieving, or puréeing ingredients. The result of this process is a meat mixture that can be smooth or textured and coarse, and that will hold together when sliced. There are four basic forcemeat styles: straight, country, gratin, and mousseline. The production and shaping methods are different for each.

Good forcemeats require a judicious use of salt and seasonings. Salt draws out the proteins in the meat and it adds a unique flavor. Classic forcemeat recipes typically call for ground spices, including quatre épices, a combination of pepper, nutmeg, allspice, and cinnamon.

Additional seasoning may include various herbs, aromatic vegetables, such as onions or mushrooms, wines, Cognacs, grain-based spirits, or vinegars. A thoroughly chilled reduction that includes garlic or shallots, herbs, wines, glace de viande or volaille, and other flavoring ingredients can also be added to forcemeats.

Mousseline is very light forcemeat and is usually based on white meats, such as veal or poultry, or fish. This is a popular choice for forcemeat hors d'oeuvre. Cream and eggs give mousseline its characteristic light texture and consistency. To prepare mousseline forcemeat, dice the main ingredients and grind them in a food processor, or grind the main ingredients through a coarse or medium plate in a meat grinder before processing with an egg white.

To make aspic-bound terrines, carefully season and prepare the main ingredients, and then add aspic as needed to bind the major ingredients. The base liquid needs to be rich and full flavored. To prepare an aspic that has superior strength, use clear stocks, broths, consommés, juices, or wines—in combination or singularly.

SERVING AND GARNISHING TERRINES AND PÂTÉS

When prepared and served with appropriate garnish, the members of the forcemeat family are appealing and hearty additions to any hors d'oeuvre menu. It is easier for guests to serve themselves presliced terrines rather than what often amounts to "digging" the slices out of earthenware dishes with the terrines still in them, as they are sometimes served. If the terrines are served sliced, the presentation can be simple or nothing short of spectacular.

Traditional terrine garnishes include portions of the poultry breast, pork, beef, veal, or lamb tenderloin; nuts (especially pistachios and pine nuts); mushrooms; truffles; and diced foie gras. The addition of garnishes can be accomplished in one of two ways: simply fold the garnish into the forcemeat (known as internal or random garnishes), or arrange the garnish into the forcemeat as you fill the mold or lay it out for a roulade or galantine (known as inlays or centered garnishes). Carefully shape and place the garnish so that each slice of the terrine has a uniform, consistent appearance.

AT LEFT: *Mushroom Salad (back, page 146), Roasted Beet Salad (middle, page 147), and Hearts of Artichoke Salad (front, page 144)*

AT RIGHT: *Mozzarella, Prosciutto, and Roasted Tomato Terrine (page 149)*

Antipasto

Literally translated from Italian, antipasto means "before the meal," just as hors d'oeuvre is French for "outside the work (meal)." The variety of foods that may be used as antipasto—collectively called antipasti—make it an easy to offer something for everyone, even those with the most difficult dietary constraints.

There are no hard and fast rules that dictate what is to be contained on a platter of antipasto. Generally an antipasto platter contains three elements: meats, cheeses, and marinated or roasted vegetables. Good, crusty Italian bread is an important accompaniment. Other items often included may be fish or seafood, nuts, and fresh and dried fruits.

Antipasti are prepared and served for easy serving and eating. Individual and bite-size elements (e.g., an assortment of sliced salami and marinated baby mozzarella cheese) or salads (e.g., marinated roasted peppers or tomatoes) make an enticing, "help-yourself" display on platters or in bowls.

Planning a selection of antipasto is the perfect opportunity to put foods together quickly that will look attractive, taste good together, and won't require cooking. Jarred marinated items, such as artichokes, roasted peppers, sun-dried tomatoes, pepperoncini, mushrooms, etc.—the list is endless—are some items to keep in the pantry for antipasto. Find a favorite brand and stick with it; the flavor and quality will vary widely.

If the flavor of jarred marinated foods isn't appealing, purchase them prepared from an Italian deli, or make your own from canned or jarred brine-packed vegetables. Rinse them thoroughly, cut them into strips, halves, or quarters (whatever size and shape the food needs to be finger- or fork-ready), and add a homemade dressing. It is best to allow the salad to marinate for at least 1 hour before serving. In a time crunch, even better, make it a day or two in advance—it will only make it taste all the better.

To serve meats for an antipasto, slice them thinly and roll them up or toss them in with a marinated vegetable salad. The meats most commonly used are cured and include but are not limited to:

- *Sopressata*

- *Genoa salami*

- *Mortadella*

- *Prosciutto*

To select cheeses for antipasto, pick one or more favorite cheeses no matter their country of origin, but to be traditional, look for a selection from Italy, such as these:

- *Marinated mozzarella*

- *Asiago*

- *Ricotta salata*

- *Robiola*

- *Pecorino Romano*

- *Parmigiano-Reggiano*

The cheeses may be served sliced or whole depending on your preference and the type of cheese. Soft ripened cheeses such as Brie or Camembert should not be served presliced. Blue cheeses are also difficult to serve sliced because of their crumbly texture. Serve cheeses whole on a cutting block or sliced and arranged on a platter or tossed with a marinated vegetable salad.

Antipasti de Salumi

T HIS TYPE of antipasto is easy to make and always pleases a crowd. If some of the specific types of meats listed here are not available, use any type of cured meats, but to keep it authentic make sure they are Italian in origin.

16 slices prosciutto di Parma or Serrano ham

16 slices coppacola

16 slices bresaola

16 slices mortadella

16 slices sopressata

1 lb fresh mozzarella, sliced

4 oz aged provolone, cubed

¼ cup extra-virgin olive oil

1 large lemon, juiced

¼ tsp freshly ground pepper

1 piece (about 1 oz) Parmigiano-Reggiano, cut into thin shavings (use a vegetable peeler)

1 cup mixed olives, for garnish

1 cup roasted peppers, for garnish

1. Arrange the meats, mozzarella, and provolone on separate plates or in groups on a platter.

2. Drizzle the olive oil over the bresaola and sprinkle with lemon juice and pepper. Top with Parmigiano-Reggiano. Garnish with olives and red peppers.

Grilled Vegetable Antipasti

A PLATTER OF grilled vegetables is a welcome addition to any event from a sit-down dinner to an hors d'oeuvre buffet. Many different vegetables grill well. Mix up the selection by substituting with unexpected items such as Belgian endive, fennel, or radicchio. Prepare the vegetables properly so that they will have ample contact with the marinade. Leafy heads such as endive or radicchio should be quartered whole, while a vegetable such as fennel should be cleaned and trimmed with the bulb sliced lengthwise.

½ cup olive oil

¼ cup balsamic vinegar

1 large lemon, juiced

2 Tbsp minced garlic

2 Tbsp minced basil

2 Tbsp minced parsley

2 Tbsp minced oregano

½ tsp minced thyme

½ tsp salt

½ tsp red pepper flakes

8 oz eggplant, trimmed and cut lengthwise into ½-in slices

8 oz zucchini, trimmed and cut lengthwise into ½-in slices

8 oz yellow squash, trimmed and cut lengthwise into ½-in slices

1 medium red onion, peeled and sliced into ½-in rings

1 small yellow pepper, cut in half lengthwise

½ cup Pecorino Romano shavings (shaved with a vegetable peeler)

chiffonade of basil

Rusks (recipe follows), for serving

1. In a large bowl, make the marinade by whisking together the oil, vinegar, lemon juice, garlic, basil, parsley, oregano, thyme, salt, and red pepper flakes. Place the eggplant, zucchini, squash, onions, and pepper in a large bowl and toss with the marinade to coat. Marinate for 1 hour.

2. Preheat a grill to high heat. Remove the vegetables from the marinade and lay on the grill in batches. Grill until marked and tender, about 3 minutes per side. Remove with tongs and place on a platter to cool slightly.

3. Sprinkle the vegetables with the cheese and basil. Serve with the rusks or as a salad.

RUSKS

MAKES 6 SERVINGS

FOR FULL potency of flavor, don't make these too far in advance. If you make them after your guests have arrived, your kitchen will be flooded with eager mouths salivating from the aroma.

1 loaf Italian bread, such as ciabatta, cut crosswise into ½-in slices, ends discarded

1 large garlic clove, peeled and crushed

Preheat the grill to medium-high. Place the bread slices on the grill and cook until marked and lightly toasted, about 1 minute per side. Rub the toasted side of the bread with the crushed garlic and reserve until ready to serve.

Seafood Antipasti

MAKES 6 SERVINGS

*T*O OFFER this antipasti as an appetizer rather than as an hors d'oeuvre, serve it as a salad on a bed of baby arugula or mixed greens, dressed with extra-virgin olive oil and sea salt.

6 small calamari, cleaned and gutted, cut crosswise into rings

12 large shrimp (16/20 count), peeled and deveined

1 lobster (1½ lb)

1 cup dry white wine

12 small mussels, bearded and scrubbed

12 littleneck clams, bearded and scrubbed

1 cup extra-virgin olive oil

2 lemons, zested and juiced

1 Tbsp red pepper flakes

½ cup finely chopped flat-leaf parsley

GARNISH

2 lemons, cut into wedges

1. Cut the squid bodies into ¼-in-wide rings. Clean and devein the shrimp.

2. Bring 6 quarts of salted water to a boil. Fill a large bowl half full with ice water.

3. Cook the shrimp in the boiling water until it is firm and opaque, 1½ minutes. Remove the shrimp with a slotted spoon and transfer to the ice water. Once the water has returned to a boil, add the calamari and cook for 1 minute, remove with a slotted spoon, and transfer to the ice water.

4. Cook the lobster for 8 minutes and then cool in the ice bath. When cool, break down and remove the meat from the tail and claws. Cut into bite-size pieces.

5. In a deep pot, bring the wine to a boil. Add the mussels and clams, cover the pan, and let the seafood steam over low heat, removing each shellfish as it opens, until they are all cooked, about 5 minutes for the mussels and 8 minutes for the clams. Discard any shellfish that do not open.

6. Whisk together the oil, lemon juice, red pepper flakes, and parsley.

7. Arrange all the seafood on a big platter and drizzle with the oil mixture. Garnish with lemon wedges.

Vegetable and Tofu Antipasti

MAKES 6 SERVINGS

*T*OFU IS a welcome addition to the traditional flavors of this salad. Marinated and broiled, it adds a certain depth of flavor as well as a satisfying texture. However, for a different profile of flavors, substitute the tofu with chicken or shrimp.

DRESSING

¼ cup red wine vinegar

1 Tbsp minced garlic

¼ cup extra-virgin olive oil

salt to taste

freshly ground pepper to taste

1 Tbsp chopped basil

2 tsp chopped oregano

MARINATED MUSHROOMS AND TOFU

¼ cup olive oil

¼ cup balsamic vinegar

1 Tbsp minced garlic

1 Tbsp chopped basil

1 tsp sea salt

1 tsp freshly ground pepper

2 portobello mushrooms, stem and gills removed

1 lb firm tofu, drained, sliced into ½-in pieces

SALAD

1 red pepper, roasted and julienned

1 yellow pepper, roasted and julienned

1 green pepper, roasted and julienned

1 bunch asparagus, blanched and cut into 1-in pieces

1 large red onion, julienned

½ cup sun-dried tomatoes, soaked in warm water and halved

¼ cup kalamata olives, pitted and cut in half

¼ cup pepperoncini, seeded and cut in half

2 Tbsp basil chiffonade

1 Tbsp whole capers

1 Tbsp minced garlic

½ Tbsp chopped oregano

1. For the dressing: Put the vinegar and garlic in a bowl. Add the olive oil slowly while whisking. Whisk in the salt and pepper, fold in the herbs, and set aside.

2. For the marinated mushrooms and tofu: Whisk together the olive oil, balsamic vinegar, garlic, basil, sea salt, and pepper in a shallow baking dish. Add the mushrooms and tofu to the marinade and toss to coat. Set aside for 30 minutes.

3. Preheat the broiler. Place the marinated mushrooms and tofu in an ovenproof pan and place under the broiler until the tofu begins to brown, about 15 minutes.

4. Remove the tofu and mushrooms from the baking pan and place them in a large serving bowl. Add all the salad ingredients to the bowl with the mushrooms and tofu. Pour the dressing over the mixture and stir gently. Chill the salad before serving.

Chili-Roasted Peanuts with Dried Cherries

MAKES 1 LB

RAISINS CAN be used instead of cherries, but the sweet-tart flavor and plump juicy flesh of the cherries make the mixture extra special and are well worth the expense.

2 Tbsp unsalted butter

1 lb raw unsalted peanuts

1 Tbsp mild chili powder

2 tsp ground cumin

2 tsp ground white pepper

2 tsp salt

½ tsp dried oregano

½ tsp cayenne

8 oz dried cherries

1. Melt the butter in a small saucepan. Add the peanuts and stir to coat with the melted butter.

2. Mix together the chili powder, cumin, pepper, salt, oregano, and cayenne in a small bowl; reserve.

3. Place the peanuts on a large sheet pan and lightly toast in a preheated 300°F oven for about 10 minutes, shaking the pan occasionally. Transfer the peanuts to a large bowl and coat with the dry ingredients. Mix in the cherries until uniformly blended.

STORAGE: Store the nut mixture in an airtight container.

AT RIGHT, CLOCKWISE, STARTING AT FRONT:
Chili-Roasted Peanuts with Dried Cherries, Spicy
Curried Cashews (page 132), and toasted almonds

Spicy Curried Cashews

MAKES 1 LB

*A*DD ECLECTIC international flair to the hors d'oeuvre table with this mixture of spices and nuts. It is an example of quintessential Indian flavors and ingredients.

1 lb whole raw cashews

2 Tbsp unsalted butter, melted

½ tsp salt

1 Tbsp curry powder

¼ tsp garlic powder

¼ tsp onion powder

pinch of cayenne

1. Toss the cashews and melted butter together on a sheet pan until evenly coated. Combine the salt and spices in a small bowl. Reserve.

2. Bake the cashews in a preheated 350°F oven until golden brown. Remove the pan with the cashews from the oven, sprinkle with the combined spices, and toss while still warm until coated. Cool before serving.

STORAGE: Store in an airtight container for up to 10 days.

CURRY POWDER

Curry powder is a combination of various spices including black pepper, cloves, cinnamon, coriander, fenugreek, cardamom, cumin, ginger, chili powder, turmeric, and nutmeg. Make your own curry powder by varying the quantities of these spices to suit your own preferences.

These Spicy Curried Cashews make an excellent bar food or addition to a buffet table. The same curry mixture from the cashew recipe can be used to flavor popcorn, other nuts, pretzels, and dried fruit. A combination of all these ingredients makes a delicious and very unique trail mix.

Spiced Mixed Nuts

MAKES 1 LB

A MIXTURE OF raw unsalted nuts can be difficult to find. To make a mixture, buy 4 ounces each of raw peanuts, almonds, pistachios, and pecans.

3 Tbsp butter

1 Tbsp Worcestershire sauce

1 lb unsalted whole raw mixed nuts

½ tsp celery seed

½ tsp garlic powder

½ tsp chili powder

¼ tsp ground cumin

pinch of cayenne

½ tsp salt

1. Melt the butter in a medium saucepan over medium heat. Add the Worcestershire sauce, mix until blended, and bring to a simmer. Add the nuts and toss well to coat evenly.

2. Mix the spices and salt in a small bowl. Sprinkle the spice mixture over the nuts and toss well to coat evenly.

3. Place the nuts on a nonstick or well-greased sheet pan and bake in a preheated 375°F oven, stirring occasionally, until evenly browned, 10 to 12 minutes. Cool completely before serving.

STORAGE: Store in an airtight container for up to 2 weeks.

Roasted Pepper Salad

MAKES 15 SERVINGS (½ CUP EACH)

REPLACE THE cilantro with flat-leaf parsley and omit the jalapeño for a more traditional Italian-style salad. Serve it as the centerpiece of your antipasto table, or in an attractive bowl alongside a cheese board.

12 oz roasted red peppers, peeled and seeded
(4 peppers)

12 oz roasted green peppers, peeled and seeded
(4 peppers)

12 oz roasted yellow peppers, peeled and seeded
(4 peppers)

DRESSING

1¼ cups Balsamic Vinaigrette (recipe follows)

1 cup julienned red onions

½ cup slivered pitted black olives, cut into strips
(20 each)

½ bunch cilantro, leaves only, chopped

1 jalapeño, minced

2 garlic cloves, minced

GARNISH

wedge of Parmigiano-Reggiano cheese

3 Tbsp toasted pine nuts

1. Cut the roasted peppers into ½-in strips.

2. Combine the dressing ingredients and pour over the peppers.

3. Toss to combine. Let the salad marinate at room temperature for 30 to 45 minutes before serving, or cover and refrigerate until needed. Let the salad come to room temperature before serving.

4. To assemble the salad, just before serving, shave curls of cheese from the wedge over each portion and top with toasted pine nuts.

NOTE: This dish can be served as a salad or as a healthy alternative to traditional high-fat sauces with grilled meats, fish, and poultry.

BALSAMIC VINAIGRETTE

MAKES 4 CUPS

IF USING good-quality balsamic vinegar, omit the red wine vinegar as it will overwhelm the mellow tones of the balsamic vinegar. Keep a jar of this vinaigrette in the refrigerator; its well-rounded, uncomplicated flavor marries well with almost any salad or sandwich.

½ cup red wine vinegar

½ cup balsamic vinegar

3 cups mild olive oil or canola oil

2 tsp salt

½ tsp ground black pepper

3 Tbsp minced herbs, such as chives, parsley, tarragon
(optional)

1. Combine the vinegars in a bowl.

2. Whisk in the oil gradually.

3. Season with the salt and pepper. Add fresh herbs, if desired.

AT LEFT: Roasted Pepper Salad (front), Marinated Tomatoes (middle, page 143), and Marinated Olives (back, page 142)

Asian Noodle Salad

THE FRESH appearance and crisp texture of this salad make it well suited for an afternoon buffet and its variety of colors will brighten any table. Its delicate flavors complement almost any dish.

1 package (8 oz) cellophane noodles (¹⁄₁₆-in thick)

2 Tbsp dark sesame oil

1 lb fresh shiitake mushrooms, stems removed and julienned

4 green onions, thinly sliced on the bias

2 carrots, peeled and cut into fine julienne

1 red pepper, cut into fine julienne

DRESSING

1 garlic clove, minced

¼ cup rice wine vinegar

1 Tbsp dark sesame oil

1 Tbsp mirin

1 Tbsp soy sauce

2 tsp minced lemongrass (inner part)

1 tsp hot bean paste

salt to taste

freshly ground pepper to taste

5 oz vegetable oil

1. Put the noodles in a bowl, cover with boiling water, and set aside to soak until softened, 8 to 10 minutes. Drain well and reserve.

2. Heat 2 Tbsp sesame oil in a sauté pan over medium heat and cook the shiitakes until softened. Place in a large bowl, cover, and refrigerate until chilled.

3. Add the green onions, carrots, pepper, and noodles to the mushrooms and toss to mix.

4. Just before serving, combine the garlic, vinegar, sesame oil, mirin, soy sauce, lemongrass, bean paste, salt, and pepper in a medium bowl and whisk until blended. Gradually add the vegetable oil, whisking until the dressing is smooth. Pour the dressing over the mushroom mixture, toss to coat, and serve.

Buckwheat Noodle Salad

To MAKE this salad look as appealing as it tastes, do not overcook the noodles and run them under cold water immediately after draining. If cooked even slightly too long, buckwheat noodles become pasty and easily break into small pieces, making the salad much less attractive.

1 lb buckwheat noodles

2 Tbsp dark sesame oil

1 lb fresh shiitake mushrooms, stems removed and caps julienned

2 Tbsp peanut oil

2 Tbsp tamari

½ tsp salt or more to taste

¼ tsp freshly ground pepper or more to taste

¼ cup mixed black and white sesame seeds

2 bunches green onions, trimmed and thinly sliced on the bias

2 carrots, peeled and cut into fine julienne

4 oz snow peas, julienned

¼ cup pickled ginger, julienned

Tahini-Soy Dressing (recipe follows)

1. Add the buckwheat noodles to a pot of boiling water and cook until tender, 1 to 2 minutes. Drain the noodles in a colander and rinse under cold running water until thoroughly chilled. Drain well and pour into a large bowl. Add 2 Tbsp sesame oil and toss to coat to prevent the noodles from sticking.

2. Sauté the mushrooms in the peanut oil until fully cooked, about 2 minutes. Add the tamari, salt, and black pepper to the mushrooms. Scrape the mixture into a bowl, cover, and refrigerate until cold.

3. Roast the black and white sesame seeds together on a sheet pan in a preheated 350°F oven until the white sesame seeds are golden brown, about 3 minutes.

4. Add the mushrooms, sesame seeds, green onions, carrots, snow peas, and ginger to the noodles. Add the dressing and toss to mix and coat. Adjust the seasoning with salt and pepper to taste and serve.

TAHINI-SOY DRESSING

MAKES 1 CUP

THIS DRESSING would be delicious on a mixed green salad. In addition, you can make this dressing in advance and refrigerate it for up to one week.

2 limes, juiced

1 shallot, minced

1 chipotle pepper, minced

½ cup vegetable oil

¼ cup tamari

¼ cup sherry vinegar

2 Tbsp tahini

2 Tbsp dark sesame oil

2 tsp minced ginger

1 tsp light brown sugar

1 tsp molasses

Combine all the ingredients in a bowl and whisk to mix well. Store the dressing in the refrigerator until ready to use.

Fattoush
(Eastern Mediterranean Bread Salad)

UNLIKE TRADITIONAL Fattoush, this salad contains more greens than bread, making it easier to prepare as well as resulting in a lighter and more nutritious dish.

8 (8-inch) pitas

3 Tbsp extra-virgin olive oil

½ tsp salt

¼ tsp freshly ground pepper

4 plum tomatoes, peeled, seeded, and cut into medium dice

1 yellow pepper, cut into small dice

2 hearts of romaine lettuce, cleaned and rough chopped

5 radishes, thinly sliced

1 European cucumber, peeled, seeded, and cut into medium dice

3 bunches green onions, chopped

½ cup mint leaves, chopped

½ cup chopped parsley

DRESSING

1 garlic clove, minced

1 lemon, juiced

¼ cup red wine vinegar

1 Tbsp chopped fresh thyme

1 tsp sugar

pinch of cayenne

salt to taste

freshly ground pepper to taste

½ cup extra-virgin olive oil

1. Cut the pitas into small wedges and put them in a large bowl. Toss with the olive oil, salt, and pepper. Spread out the pitas on a sheet pan and bake in a preheated 300°F oven until crisp but not crumbled, about 25 minutes, turning them halfway through the baking time. Allow to cool completely.

2. Combine the tomatoes, pepper, lettuce, radishes, cucumber, green onions, mint, and parsley in a large bowl.

3. Make the dressing: Combine the garlic, lemon juice, vinegar, thyme, sugar, cayenne, salt, and pepper in a medium bowl and whisk until blended. Gradually mix in the oil, whisking until blended and smooth. Pour the dressing over the vegetable salad and toss until mixed. Add the pita bread and toss to coat. Adjust the seasoning if necessary with salt and pepper. If the salad is dry, sprinkle it with a little water to moisten.

Mushrooms à la Grecque

TIMELESS AND delicious, this salad can be made in a flash and is an excellent complement to almost any menu, whether the flavors are warm and rich or bright and fresh. It also holds well so make it a couple of days in advance to help alleviate the day-of-the-party rush.

3 (10-oz) packages whole button mushrooms, cleaned and trimmed

3 garlic cloves, minced

1 very large sachet with fresh thyme, basil, fresh bay leaves, and parsley stems

¾ cup white wine vinegar

½ cup extra-virgin olive oil

¼ cup water

3 Tbsp honey

1 Tbsp salt or more to taste

½ tsp red pepper flakes

HERBS TO GARNISH

3 Tbsp chopped parsley

1 Tbsp basil chiffonade

2 tsp chopped thyme

1. Combine the mushrooms, garlic, sachet, vinegar, oil, water, honey, 1 Tbsp salt, and red pepper flakes in a stainless-steel saucepan. Stir until the salt dissolves and then bring to a boil.

2. Cover with a lid and simmer 6 to 8 minutes.

3. To serve, drain the mushrooms slightly from their liquid. Add the fresh herbs and check seasonings, adding more salt if needed.

Roasted Peppers with Capers and Cumin

MAKES 8 SERVINGS

*T*HESE PEPPERS are excellent served warm or at room temperature with freshly warmed pita wedges and additional chopped flat-leaf parsley. For more flavor, make them in advance to allow more time to marinate in the dressing.

3 red peppers

3 yellow peppers

3 green peppers

6 Tbsp extra-virgin olive oil

2 large onions, sliced with the grain

6 garlic cloves, peeled and slivered

4 Tbsp capers, rinsed and roughly chopped

1 tsp ground cumin

¼ cup balsamic vinegar

4 Tbsp chopped parsley

2 Tbsp chopped thyme

1 tsp salt

½ tsp freshly ground pepper

1. Broil the peppers on a sheet pan until charred on all sides, turning with tongs. Put the peppers in a brown paper bag, seal, and steam for 30 minutes. Remove the seeds, stems, and peel. Cut the peppers into strips and put them into a large bowl.

2. Pour the olive oil into a sauté pan over medium heat, add the onions and garlic, and cook until lightly caramelized, about 8 minutes.

3. Add the onion mixture, capers, cumin, vinegar, parsley, thyme, salt, and pepper to the peppers and mix well. Taste and add more salt and pepper if needed.

Thai Seafood Salad

*I*T IS the chili paste that makes this dish come alive. The chili paste is aromatic and mellow, which gives this salad a full-bodied flavor.

4 tsp Thai chili paste

¼ cup Thai fish sauce or more to taste

¼ cup lime juice or more to taste

1 Tbsp sugar

3 Thai bird chiles, minced

2 stalks lemongrass, minced

3 shallots, sliced thin

1 lb shrimp, (21/25 count), peeled, deveined, and cut lengthwise

2 lb squid, cleaned, bodies cut crosswise into ¼-in-thick rings, and tentacles cut into bite-size pieces

¾ cup mint leaves, coarsely chopped, plus 15 leaves, halved, for garnish

¼ cup shredded cilantro

1. Whisk together the chili paste, fish sauce, lime juice, sugar, chiles, lemongrass, and shallots in a small bowl. Set aside.

2. Bring two pots of salted water to a bare simmer (190°F). Add the shrimp to one pan, stir to separate, and cook until the shrimp become opaque and curl, about 1 minute. Add the squid to the second pot, stir to separate, and cook until the rings are white and opaque, 1 minute.

3. Immediately lift the seafood from the simmering water with a slotted spoon or skimmer. Add the seafood to the dressing mixture while it is still very hot. Turn the seafood in the dressing. Add the mint and cilantro to the salad and toss to distribute evenly. Season with additional fish sauce or lemon juice as needed.

4. Serve the salad at room temperature.

Marinated Olives

MAKES 3 LB

Manzanillas, Gordalis, Niçoise, Kalamata, Atalanti, Picholine, Amfissa, and Nafplion are all fine choices for olives. If it is difficult to find a variety, just use black and green to get some color variation in the dish.

1 lb mixed olives

2 Tbsp dried oregano, preferably Italian wild mountain or Greek

1 Tbsp rosemary leaves

1 Tbsp thyme leaves

1 Tbsp marjoram leaves

1 tsp red pepper flakes

2 lemons or oranges

extra-virgin olive oil to moisten olive mixture

1. Spread out the olives on paper towels and blot dry to remove most of the brine.

2. Put the olives, herbs, and pepper flakes in a bowl and grate the zest from the lemons or oranges on top. Sprinkle with extra-virgin olive oil to moisten and toss to mix well. Add more oil if needed.

OLIVES

Olives make a quick but elegant hors d'oeuvre and are a key ingredient in tapenades and antipastos. Olives are generally found in three color categories: green, back, or blond. For an hors d'oeuvre or as an accompaniment to a cheese platter, choose either pitted or unpitted olives. Use unpitted olives for making tapenades or garnishing salads. Explore the olive bar at your local grocery store to discover new types of olives. Here are some that are particularly flavorful when marinated:

- *Kalamata: strong flavor, high acidity and salt content*

- *Niçoise: slightly sour flavor*

- *Picholine: fresh and slightly nutty flavor, maintain their texture when cured and marinated*

- *Sicilian: green, sour olive, often marinated with herbs*

- *Cerignola: large, green olive from Italy, sweet flavor*

Marinated Tomatoes

USE A single variety of tomato or a combination in this salad. Even better, use heirloom varieties—their colors and shapes make a beautiful presentation. If the tomato skins are thin and tender, peeling is optional.

2 lb tomatoes

DRESSING

⅓ cup extra-virgin olive oil

3 Tbsp red wine vinegar

1½ Tbsp basil chiffonade

1½ Tbsp chopped marjoram

1 tsp salt

½ tsp ground black pepper

1. Peel the tomatoes, if desired, and cut in halves, quarters, or wedges, depending on the size of the tomatoes, to make large bite-size pieces.

2. Combine the dressing ingredients in a large bowl.

3. Add the tomatoes to the dressing, toss to coat, and let stand at room temperature 2 hours before serving.

NOTE: Tomatoes lose flavor when exposed to cold temperatures. For this reason, this salad should not be refrigerated before serving.

TOMATO VARIETIES

The summer season produces the juiciest and most flavorful tomatoes. Because they're left on the vine longer, vine-ripened tomatoes tend to have more flavor than tomatoes that are picked green. Slicing tomatoes, such as the beefsteak, are sturdy tomatoes excellent for sandwiches and grilling. Heirloom tomatoes, which are open-pollinated tomatoes, have become increasingly popular. They are often found in different shapes and colors, such as white, purple, and striped. Grown for optimum flavor and texture rather than shipping capabilities, heirloom tomatoes are ideal for marinating. They are more expensive than regular tomatoes, but the flavor is often worth the extra cost. Heirloom tomatoes can be found at farmers' markets and in upscale grocery stores.

Hearts of Artichoke Salad

*I*F PREP time is at a premium or if fresh artichokes are unavailable, use canned artichokes. Although they will not have the same creamy rich flavor and texture, the lively mix of the other salad ingredients will make this salad refreshing.

2 lemons, halved

10 artichoke hearts, quartered, or 30 baby artichokes

DRESSING

1 cup olive oil

½ cup balsamic vinegar

salt to taste

ground white pepper to taste

½ bunch flat-leaf parsley, leaves only, chopped

30 Kalamata olives, pitted

1 red onion, sliced into thin rings or julienne

4 lb plum tomatoes, peeled, seeded, and quartered

1. Squeeze the juice from the lemons into a large bowl. Add the lemon halves and about 4 cups cold water. Working with 1 artichoke at a time, cut the ends off the artichokes and trim off the outer leaves. Scoop out the chokes and quarter each heart. Put the heart pieces in the bowl of lemon (called *acidulated*) water to prevent discoloration.

2. Simmer the artichoke hearts until tender, 8 to 12 minutes. Drain and let dry on paper towels while preparing the dressing.

3. Whisk all the dressing ingredients in a bowl. Add the artichoke hearts, olives, onions, and tomatoes and toss to coat.

4. Let the salad stand at room temperature for at least 30 minutes before serving.

AT RIGHT: Hearts of Artichoke Salad (front), Roasted Beet Salad (middle, page 147), and Mushroom Salad (back, page 146)

Mushroom Salad

*I*F WILD mushrooms aren't in season, there are several cultivated exotic varieties that would work well in this salad. Chanterelle, oyster, and shiitake are three of the more commonly available cultivated exotics.

½ cup olive oil

1 lb cremini mushrooms, quartered

1 lb white mushrooms, quartered

2 lb assorted wild mushrooms

1 Tbsp minced garlic

½ cup minced shallots

2 Tbsp minced marjoram

2 Tbsp minced parsley

2 Tbsp minced mint

⅓ cup lemon juice

3 Tbsp sherry vinegar

2 Tbsp truffle oil

2 tsp salt

¼ tsp ground black pepper

1. Heat 1 Tbsp of the oil in a large sauté pan over high heat. Add half the cremini, white, and wild mushrooms and sauté until lightly browned and cooked through, 5 to 7 minutes. Transfer to a mixing bowl. Repeat with the remaining mushrooms, adding more oil as needed. Let the mushrooms cool.

2. Combine the garlic, shallots, marjoram, parsley, mint, lemon juice, vinegar, truffle oil, salt, pepper, and the remaining olive oil in a bowl and whisk until blended.

3. Pour the vinaigrette over the mushrooms and toss to coat. Cover and refrigerate for at least 2 hours or up to 24 hours prior to serving.

Roasted Beet Salad

MAKES 20 SERVINGS

USE RED or golden beets for this salad. The beets are roasted in this recipe, but could also be boiled or steamed. For a special presentation, alternate the sliced beets with orange slices.

8 beets, greens trimmed to 1 in

1½ tsp kosher salt

DRESSING

⅓ cup extra-virgin olive oil

2 Tbsp red wine vinegar

2 Tbsp lemon juice

pinch of salt or more to taste

pinch of cayenne

1. Arrange the beets in a baking dish or pan and add water just to cover the bottom. Season the beets with salt, cover with foil, and roast in a preheated 375°F oven until fork-tender, about 1 hour, depending on size.

2. While the beets are roasting, combine all the dressing ingredients in a large bowl and whisk until blended.

3. Trim the beets, slip off the skins, and slice into rounds. Add the beets to the dressing while they are still warm and toss to coat.

4. Let the beet salad stand at room temperature for at least 30 minutes before serving or cover and refrigerate until serving.

BEETS

Beets have a slightly sweet, earthy flavor and add gorgeous color to any dish. Roasting brings out the sweetness and deep flavors in beets, but they can also be steamed, boiled, and pickled. Roasted beets, served either hot or cold, pair well with fennel, orange, fresh ginger, and honey.

Besides the traditional red beet, there are golden beets, white beets, and candy-striped beets. Baby beets are sweeter than the larger varieties and cook more quickly. Beets belong to the tuber family and are therefore available all year round, although the quality varies greatly between the seasons.

Mozzarella, Prosciutto, and Roasted Tomato Terrine

MAKES ABOUT 20 SERVINGS

*I*MPRESSIVE AND intricate as this terrine appears, it is much less challenging to make than one would think. To keep the individual layers clearly defined, clean off the knife after cutting each slice.

3 lb plum tomatoes

½ cup basil chiffonade

¼ cup olive oil

2 tsp salt

1 tsp ground black pepper

8 oz fresh spinach pasta dough or cooked lasagna sheets

12 oz fresh cheese curd

8 oz very thinly sliced prosciutto

1. Cut the tomatoes into ¼-in-thick slices and lay them on a rack set in a roasting pan. Season the tomatoes with the basil, oil, salt, and pepper and dry in a preheated 200°F oven until slightly dry, shriveled, and tacky to the touch, 2 to 3 hours. Cool and reserve.

2. While the tomatoes roast, prepare the spinach pasta. Roll the pasta into a ⅛-in-thick sheet and cut into pieces the size of the bottom of a 12 × 4 × 3-in terrine mold.

3. Bring 3 qt of salted water to a simmer in a large pot, add the spinach pasta sheets, and cook until tender, 2 to 3 minutes. Drain, refresh in cold water, and drain again. Reserve until needed.

4. To prepare fresh mozzarella using fresh cheese curd, roll and stretch the mozzarella into sheets (⅛ in thick) and trim as necessary to the size of the pasta sheets.

5. Line the terrine mold with plastic wrap, leaving an overhang. To assemble the terrine, put 1 pasta sheet on the bottom of the terrine, cover with one-fourth of the prosciutto, then one-fourth of the mozzarella, and cover with one-fourth of the roasted tomatoes. Repeat the process until the ingredients are used up and the mold is filled (there should be 4 layers of each ingredient). Finish with a layer of pasta, fold the plastic wrap over, and smooth the top. Cover the terrine with a lid and bake in a water bath in a preheated 250°F oven until the layers set together slightly, about 30 minutes.

6. Weight the terrine with a 2-lb press plate and refrigerate at least overnight. The terrine is now ready to unmold, slice, and serve.

7. To unmold the finished terrine, invert it (in the mold, in the plastic wrap) onto a flat work surface. Hold one end of the plastic wrap onto the counter and lift the mold away with the other hand. To serve, place the wrapped terrine on a cutting board and cut into ⅜-in-thick slices, cutting through the plastic wrap. Remove the plastic wrap after the slices are arranged on plates or platters.

STORAGE: The terrine can be kept wrapped in plastic wrap in the refrigerator up to 3 days.

AT LEFT: This terrine can be served with a vinaigrette and green salad or French bread slices topped with Tapenade (page 47).

Roasted Vegetable Terrine
with Goat's Milk Cheese

MAKES 18 TO 20 SERVINGS

U SE A piping bag to fill the terrine with the goat's milk cheese custard—it makes it easier to distribute the custard evenly over the vegetables.

MARINADE

2 garlic cloves, minced, sautéed, and cooled

2 Tbsp olive oil plus extra for the parchment

1 Tbsp chopped flat-leaf parsley

1 Tbsp chopped chives

1 Tbsp Dijon mustard

2 tsp salt

2 tsp chopped rosemary

2 tsp anchovy paste

2 tsp honey

½ tsp ground white pepper

VEGETABLES

2 lb zucchini

2 lb yellow squash

1¼ lb eggplant

2 lb tomatoes

2 portobello mushrooms

CUSTARD

8 oz fresh goat's milk cheese

1 large egg

1. Combine the marinade ingredients in a large bowl and whisk until blended.

2. Cut all vegetables lengthwise into ⅛-in-thick slices and add to the marinade. Toss to coat.

3. Line 3 baking sheets with oiled parchment and spread out the vegetables on top in a single layer.

4. Bake the vegetables in a preheated 200°F oven until dry but not brittle, about 1 hour. Remove from the oven and cool.

5. Combine the goat's milk cheese and egg in a bowl and whisk together to make the custard.

6. Line a terrine mold with plastic wrap, leaving an overhang, and assemble the terrine by alternating layers of vegetables and the custard until the terrine is filled. Fold the plastic wrap over and smooth the top.

7. Cover the terrine with a lid and poach in a 170°F water bath in a preheated 300°F oven to an internal temperature of 145°F, about 60 minutes.

8. Remove the terrine from the water bath and let it cool.

9. If a firmer texture is desired, weight the terrine with a 2-lb press plate. Refrigerate at least overnight and up to 3 days. The terrine is now ready to unmold, slice, and serve.

10. To unmold the finished terrine, invert it (in the mold, in the plastic wrap) onto a flat work surface. Hold one end of the plastic wrap onto the counter and lift the mold away with the other hand. To serve, place the wrapped terrine on a cutting board and cut into ⅜-in-thick slices, cutting through the plastic wrap. Remove the plastic wrap after the slices are arranged on plates or platters.

STORAGE: The terrine can be kept wrapped in plastic wrap in the refrigerator up to 7 days.

NOTE: Vegetables can be marinated and grilled instead of dried.

AT RIGHT: Mozzarella, Prosciutto, and Roasted Tomato Terrine (left, page 149) and Roasted Vegetable Terrine with Goat's Milk Cheese (right)

Roasted Pepper and Eggplant Terrine

T O MAKE this terrine as impressive looking as it should, carefully cut the eggplant and peppers so that the slices are uniform and even. Otherwise, the completed terrine will look somewhat haphazard and messy.

1 lb eggplant, peeled and cut lengthwise into ¼-in-thick slices

3 lb red peppers

3 lb yellow peppers

3 lb green peppers

2 tsp salt plus extra for the eggplant

½ tsp ground black pepper

3 Tbsp powdered gelatin

1½ cups red wine vinaigrette (any kind)

1. Spread out the eggplant slices on a sheet pan lined with paper towels and sprinkle with salt. Let drain for 30 minutes and pat dry. Grill or broil the eggplant until tender and the peppers are charred on all sides. Put the peppers in a paper bag and seal. Let stand until cool enough to handle. Peel and seed the peppers. Trim the vegetables to fit a terrine mold. Season with 2 tsp salt and the pepper.

2. Sprinkle the gelatin over the vinaigrette in a small bowl and stir to break up any clumps. Let the gelatin soften in the vinaigrette for about 3 minutes. Heat the softened gelatin until the granules melt and the mixture is clear over simmering water or in a microwave for about 20 seconds on low power.

3. Line the mold with plastic wrap, leaving an overhang. Layer the peppers and eggplant alternately with the vinaigrette mixture to fill the mold. Fold the plastic wrap over the filling and smooth the top.

4. Weight the terrine with a 2-lb press plate. Refrigerate until set, at least 2 days. The terrine is now ready to unmold, slice, and serve.

5. To unmold the finished terrine, invert it (in the mold, in the plastic wrap) onto a flat work surface. Hold one end of the plastic wrap onto the counter and lift the mold away with the other hand. To serve, place the wrapped terrine on a cutting board and cut into ⅜-in-thick slices, cutting through the plastic wrap. Remove the plastic wrap after the slices are arranged on plates or platters.

STORAGE: The terrine can be kept wrapped in plastic wrap in the refrigerator up to 7 days.

Mediterranean Seafood Terrine

THE MOUSSELINE-STYLE forcemeat used in this terrine has a light and airy texture as its name suggests: mousse is the French word for "froth" or "foam." Its richness makes it a perfect choice for hors d'oeuvre, as a small portion is delightfully satisfying.

MOUSSELINE

½ cup heavy cream, infused with saffron and chilled (see Note)

2 large egg whites

4 oz shrimp, peeled, deveined, and diced

10 oz scallops, diced

2 tsp salt

½ tsp ground white pepper

GARNISH

8 oz shrimp (16/20 count), peeled, deveined, halved lengthwise, and cut crosswise into eighths

8 oz sea scallops, quartered

1 Tbsp chopped flat-leaf parsley

2 tsp chopped basil

1. To prepare the mousseline, combine the infused cream, egg whites, shrimp, scallops, salt, and pepper in a food processor and process until smooth. Scrape the mixture into a large bowl.

2. Fold the garnish ingredients into the mousseline using a rubber spatula and working over an ice bath.

3. Line a terrine mold with plastic wrap, leaving an overhang, and fill it with the mousseline. Fold over the plastic, smooth the top, and cover the terrine.

4. Poach the terrine in a 170°F water bath in a preheated 300°F oven to an internal temperature of 145°F, 20 to 25 minutes. Remove the terrine from the water bath and cool to an internal temperature of 90°F. Refrigerate the terrine overnight. The terrine is now ready to unmold, slice, and serve.

5. To unmold the finished terrine, invert it (in the mold, in the plastic wrap) onto a flat work surface. Hold one end of the plastic wrap onto the counter and lift the mold away with the other hand. To serve, place the wrapped terrine on a cutting board and cut into ⅜-in-thick slices, cutting through the plastic wrap. Remove the plastic wrap after the slices are arranged on plates or platters.

STORAGE: The terrine can be kept wrapped in plastic wrap in the refrigerator up to 3 days.

NOTE: To make the saffron-infused cream, add a pinch of saffron to 5 oz very warm heavy cream. Cover and steep until the cream turns a brilliant yellow-gold color. Refrigerate until very cold before using in the mousseline.

Quick Chicken Liver Terrine

THE EASE of this terrine, as well as its depth of flavor, is sure to make it a favorite. The ample amount of butter gives it a texture and flavor that is closer to foie gras than to simple chicken liver.

10 oz chicken livers

1 cup (2 sticks) unsalted butter

⅛ cup minced shallot

salt as needed

ground black pepper as needed

ground cinnamon as needed

ground nutmeg as needed

¼ cup dry marsala wine

¼ cup heavy cream, whipped to soft peaks

1. Clean the chicken livers of any connective tissues and set cleaned livers aside.

2. In a large sauté pan, melt the butter over medium heat and cook the shallots until translucent, about 3 minutes.

3. Add the chicken livers to the pan and cook through, about 7 minutes. Add the salt, pepper, cinnamon, nutmeg, and wine.

4. Purée the mixture in a blender or food processor. Fold in the whipped cream and pour the mixture into a 6-cup terrine. Cover with plastic wrap and refrigerate overnight.

5. Serve with crackers or toast points.

Brie Cheese Torte with Smoked Salmon and Dill

FOR THIS dish a simple piece of dental floss transforms an ordinary wheel of cheese into a beautiful dish to take center stage at a buffet table.

1 wheel Brie cheese, about 2 pounds

4 ounces smoked salmon, thinly sliced

½ bunch fresh dill, chopped

1. With unflavored dental floss, cut the wheel of Brie into three crosswise layers. On the bottom layer of Brie, place a very thin layer of smoked salmon, then top with some chopped dill.

2. Place the second layer of Brie directly on the first and repeat the process. Finish with the top layer of Brie. Coat the entire outside of the torte with dill.

3. Wrap tightly in plastic wrap and refrigerate overnight.

4. To serve, cut the torte in half to show the layers and let guests cut their own portions.

Chapter Seven

CHEESE SERVICE

❧

THERE ARE SO many cheeses available today that referencing them for classification is controversial, if not impossible. Milk type, country of origin, region, handling, aging, and texture are some of the various classification strategies that have been used. Although most experts agree that none of these classifications are completely adequate, so far no one has been able to come up with one that really covers all the variables. Even when two experts agree on which method to use, they do not necessarily agree on which cheeses fall into which categories.

For the sake of discussion, this section presents several broad groups of cheese that have been loosely categorized according to texture.

SOFT FRESH CHEESES

Soft fresh cheeses are those cheeses that are unripened and generally have a fresh, clean, creamy flavor. These cheeses are typically the most perishable and are sometimes held in brines. Examples of soft fresh cheeses are cottage cheese, pot cheese, queso blanco, and cream cheese. (Recipes for fresh cheeses appear on pages 167, 172, and 173.)

Ricotta cheese, made from recooking whey, actually began in Italy as a by-product of the cheese-making industry. (The name literally means "recook.") When whey is heated, the proteins fuse together and create a new curd that, when drained, becomes a snowy white ricotta that is high in moisture and naturally low in fat. It is commonly used in Italian cooking as a filling for pastas or as a base for cheesecakes. Today, some ricottas are made with added part-skim or whole milk for a richer flavor.

Mascarpone is a fresh cheese made by curdling heavy cream with citric acid. The process releases excess moisture and yields a rich creamy cheese that is mildly acidic and adapts to both sweet and savory preparations. One of the most famous uses of mascarpone is in the dessert tiramisù, in which the rich cheese is layered with sponge cake or ladyfingers that have been dipped in espresso and Marsala wine. Savory mascarpone dishes such as dips and spreads can also include herbs and spices.

In the United States, fresh goat's milk cheeses have become very popular and are produced in many parts of the country. They are found in a variety of shapes and are often coated in herbs or edible ash.

SOFT-RIPENED CHEESES

Cheeses that have typically been sprayed or dusted with a mold and allowed to ripen are categorized as soft-ripened. The two most popular varieties are Brie and Camembert. Neither name is protected by law, so both have been counterfeited in many places with vast differences in quality.

Soft-ripened cheeses vary in fat content. For example, single–, double–, and triple–cream cheeses contain 50, 60, and 70 percent butterfat, respectively.

Soft-ripened cheeses should be eaten only when properly ripened. An underripe cheese is firm and chalky, an overripe cheese will run when cut, and a cheese ready for eating will "bulge" when cut and barely hold its shape. Soft-ripened cheeses will ripen only until they are cut open. After that, they will begin to dry and deteriorate. To check for ripeness before cutting, press firmly but gently in the middle of the cheese—it should softly yield. An overripe cheese will emit an ammonia odor.

Serve soft-ripened cheeses at room temperature for dessert or as an appetizer. For those who are not purists, these cheeses can also be served warm by baking them in a crust of flaky dough or toasted almonds.

It still remains a matter of taste as to whether soft-ripened cheeses should be eaten with the rind. Even the "experts" don't agree on that age-old discussion, so it should be left up to the individual.

SEMI-SOFT CHEESES

Semi-soft cheeses include a wide variety ranging from mild and buttery to very pungent and aromatic. They are allowed to ripen in several ways.

RIND-RIPENED CHEESES

Wash-rind cheeses are periodically washed with brine, beer, cider, wine, brandy, or oils during the ripening period. This remoistening encourages bacterial growth, sometimes known as a "smear," which allows the cheese to ripen from the outside in. Popular examples of this type of cheese include Limburger and its famous American counterpart, Liederkranz, both of which are intensely pungent, as well as Muenster, Saint Paulin, and Port-Salut.

DRY-RIND CHEESES

Dry-rind cheeses are those that are allowed to form a natural rind during ripening. Bel Paese (Italian for "beautiful country") is a cheese of Italian origin that has become quite popular since it was first made in 1929. Its soft texture and very mild flavor have contributed to its popularity. Havarti, another popular dry-rind cheese, has a buttery flavor that is often enhanced with herbs or spices such as dill, caraway, and basil.

WAXED-RIND CHEESES

Gouda and Edam are semi-soft cheeses that are sealed in wax before the aging process. These cheeses, which get their names from two towns in Holland, have been made for eight hundred years. Gouda is made from whole milk and is softer and richer than Edam, which is made from part-skim milk and is firmer. These cheeses may be either flavored or smoked, and are available in mild and aged varieties.

BLUE-VEINED CHEESES

Blue or blue-veined cheeses are thought to have been among some of the first cheeses produced. Although there is no specific research to prove the theory, it is believed that the mold was first introduced to cheese from moldy bread that had come in contact with the cheese.

In the modern production of blue cheeses, needles are used to form holes that allow gases to escape and oxygen to enter to support mold growth within the cheese. The cheese is then salted or brined and allowed to ripen in caves or under "cave-like conditions." Some of the most famous blue cheeses are Roquefort, Gorgonzola, Stilton, and Maytag blue

Roquefort is made strictly from raw sheep's milk and has been made since ancient times in the Rouergue area of southern France. Today the cheeses are still ripened in the caves of Cambalou for three months to develop their unique character. They may be eaten after the initial ripening, but are more typically stored for an additional three to twelve months, as the market allows.

One of the things that makes Roquefort unique is the fact that the mold used to ripen it is not grown in a laboratory, as are molds for many other blue cheeses. Instead, Roquefort mold is developed naturally from rye bread. Roquefort, should, therefore, be emphasized, or at least be mentioned, whenever the cheese is served or used in cooking.

Gorgonzola is another special blue cheese. Unlike Roquefort, Gorgonzola is made from cow's milk. Its mold is from a completely different strain, which is now commercially produced. Gorgonzola is made with evening milk and the following day's morning milk. There are two varieties available: "sweet," which is aged three months; and "naturale," which is aged further and has a fuller, more robust flavor.

PASTA FILATA CHEESES

Pasta filata literally means "spun curds" or "spun paste." During manufacture, the curds are dipped into hot water and then stretched or spun until the proper consistency and texture is achieved. They are then kneaded and molded into the desired shapes.

Pasta filata cheeses are a group of cheeses that are related by the process used in their manufacture, rather than by their textures. In fact, the textures of pasta filata cheeses run the gamut from soft to hard, depending upon how they are aged, if at all.

The most common cheese of this category is mozzarella. In 1990, over 1.5 billion pounds of mozzarella were produced in America alone. Today there are two types of mozzarella available: the traditional fresh style, which is available in a variety of shapes and sizes, and the newer American invention of low-moisture mozzarella, which has a longer shelf life than the fresh style. Both whole milk and part-skim varieties are available. (The recipe for making fresh mozzarella appears on page 167.)

Provolone is another popular pasta filata cheese that is similarly handled but is made with a different culture. Once the curd is stretched and kneaded, it is rubbed with brine and tied into shape. It is then hung and left to dry in sizes ranging from 250 grams to 200 pounds. Provolone is often smoked or aged (or both) for additional character and firmer texture.

HARD CHEESES

A variety of hard cheeses are produced throughout the world, and of these, Cheddars and Swiss-style cheeses are among the most well known.

Originating in England, Cheddar has become the most popular hard cheese in the United States. The Pilgrims brought Cheddar formulas to the United States, and by 1790, it was produced in such quantities that it was exported back to England.

Cheddar derives its name from the process used in its manufacture. The "cheddaring" process involves turning and stacking the slabs of young cheese to extract more whey and give the cheese its characteristic texture. The yellow color of some Cheddars is achieved through the addition of annatto seed paste and has nothing to do with the flavor.

Once the cheddaring process is complete, the cheeses are wrapped in cheesecloth dipped in wax and allowed to ripen. Cheddars are categorized by age. Current Cheddar is aged for thirty days, mild for one to three months, medium for three to six months, sharp for six to nine months, and extra-sharp for nine months to five years.

Many cheeses that originated in the United States are produced using the cheddaring method. American cheese is said to have gotten its name after the American Revolution when the proud producers of Cheddar in the United States did not want their cheeses to be mistaken for anything that might have originated in England, and aptly labeled them "American cheese."

Colby is another truly American cheese that was invented in the town of Colby, Wisconsin, in 1874. When Colby slabs are cut in half, they are popularly known as longhorns.

Monterey Jack is also an American original cheese produced in the style of Cheddar. It was first made by David Jacks in Monterey, California, in 1849, and has remained popular to this day. Aged Jack cheese, known as dry Jack, makes an excellent grating cheese.

The cheeses generically referred to as Swiss are also hard cheeses. These cheeses are characterized by holes, sometimes called eyes, which range in size from tiny to the size of a quarter. Swiss cheeses are often mellow in flavor and have excellent melting properties. Some of the more well-known varieties of Swiss cheese include Gruyère, Emmentaler, Beaufort, and Jarlsberg.

VERY HARD CHEESES

In Italy, these cheeses are known as the granas (from the Italian word for "grain"), because of their granular texture. The most popular of these cheeses are Parmesan and Romano, which are now produced in the United States and South America, but are different from their predecessors. Very hard cheeses are most often grated or shaved, but they are also traditionally eaten in chunks broken off with a special knife.

True Parmigiano–Reggiano is often referred to as the king of cheeses. It is believed that the formula for this cheese has not changed in more than seven hundred years, and its origins date back even further. This legendary cheese is made slowly and carefully following strict guidelines that require it to be aged a minimum of fourteen months, although most are aged for twenty-four months. *Stravecchio*, or extra aged, has ripened for as long as three years.

The flavor of Parmigiano–Reggiano is complex and unique. Steven Jenkins, author of *The Cheese Primer*, describes it as "spicy like cinnamon or nutmeg; salty like liquor accompanying an oyster; sweet like ginger cookies; and nutty like black walnuts—all at the same time."

Romano cheeses—named for the city of Rome—come in several different varieties. Pecorino Romano, which is made with sheep's milk, is probably the best known. Caprino Romano is a very sharp goat's milk version, and vacchino Romano is a mild version made from cow's milk.

CHEESE SERVICE

SELECTING THE CHEESE A variety of approaches can be taken when developing a cheese board. Cheeses should be selected based on color, shape, texture, richness, and intensity. A modest selection might simply include a single cheese of the best quality from the soft, blue, and hard categories. More extensive selections continue to build their offerings by expanding selections within categories and developing a special selection to feature local or regional favorites.

Cheese plates, boards, or carts often contain a variety of cheeses, but sometimes it is interesting to compose a board that features only one type of milk, sometimes referred to as a flight of cheeses, in the same way that a flight of Chardonnays or Pinot Noirs might be offered. A sheep's milk cheese board, for instance, gives the guest a chance to taste and compare a variety of cheeses made from the same main ingredient. This is an opportunity that many people have never had, but would probably be interested in trying.

PRESENTING THE CHEESE Cheeses should be allowed to come to room temperature before they are served. This process, known as aromatization, brings out the fullest flavor of the cheese, so that all its nuances can be enjoyed.

STYLES OF PRESENTATION Cheeses may be served as a course in and of themselves, often preceding, or in place of dessert. In à la carte service, some restaurants present their customers with a cheese cart from which they may sample a variety of cheeses. The customer chooses which cheeses he or she would like to try, and their server then prepares a plate tableside, consisting of the desired cheeses, bread or crackers, and occasionally some fruit.

On a buffet, cheese boards are eye-catching items that have always been popular. The board itself can be as simple as a piece of wood, reserved strictly for cheese-board service, that has been decoratively lined with clean, nontoxic leaves. More common, however, are service platters, mirrors, or marble.

PARTNERS AND ACCOMPANIMENTS FOR CHEESE Three types of foods have a natural affinity for cheese: wine or beer, varieties of bread and crackers, and fruit. Bread is probably the original accompaniment to cheese. The combination of the two provided portable sustenance for the traveler and a convenient meal for others.

Wine, particularly tannic wine, offers a perfect contrast to the richness of cheese. The wine's acidity cuts through the cheese's butterfat. Beer, on the other hand, works well to contrast the salt component of cheese, making it an ideal accompaniment.

The sweet juiciness of many fruits also pairs well with the earthy richness of cheeses. Classic examples include apples with Cheddar, and pears with blue cheese.

CARING FOR CHEESES: STORAGE AND HANDLING

Because cheese is a living food with active biological attributes, it is critical to maintain the highest standards in sanitation during handling activities. Cheese may be a potentially hazardous food, if handled improperly.

When handling cheese that is not going to be cooked, it is important to either use utensils or wear food-service gloves to prevent the contamination of the cheese with bacteria from the hands, and the formation of unsightly fingerprints on the cheese.

All food-contact areas should be cleaned and sanitized properly with hot, soapy water and sanitizing solution to prevent cross-contamination. All cheese-cutting equipment should be similarly sanitized.

If cheeses become unnaturally moldy, they may be trimmed by cutting ½ to 1 inch past the mold, being careful not to transfer the mold to the good portion.

Cheeses should never be allowed to sit out at room temperature for extended periods of time, beyond that required to aromatize the cheeses. Always keep cheeses and cheese preparations covered and refrigerated properly.

Blue Cheese Mousse

MAKES 32 SERVINGS

THIS DELICIOUS mousse looks impressive when served piped onto crackers or into endive leaves using a medium-size star tip. Garnish each bit with a snip of a fresh green herb like parsley or dill.

1 lb 4 oz blue cheese

1 lb 4 oz cream cheese

1 Tbsp kosher salt

½ tsp ground black pepper

½ cup heavy cream, whipped to soft peaks

1. Combine the blue and cream cheeses in a food processor fitted with a metal blade and process until very smooth. Add the salt and pepper and process until blended. Scrape the mixture into a large bowl.

2. Fold the whipped cream into the cheese mousse until well blended, using a rubber spatula. (There should be no lumps.)

3. Use the mousse to prepare canapés or as a filling or dip.

MOUSSES AND PÂTÉS

Mousses and pâtés can be piped to create attractive hors d'oeuvre and canapés. Prepare a piping bag with a decorative piping tip, such as a round, star, or leaf tip. Pipe the mousse onto the bases of the canapés, such as crostinis, toasted bread rounds, crackers, fresh vegetables, or smoked salmon rosettes. Ensure that the mousse is very smooth or it will be difficult to pipe. Many different varieties of cheeses can be made into mousses, such as goat's milk cheese, cream cheese, and Parmesan. In addition, seafood, vegetables, poultry, and meats make flavorful and interesting mousses.

Blue Cheese Tartlets

*F*OR THOSE who love blue cheese, these tartlets are a dream. You can control the flavor by the blue cheese you select: Danish or Maytag blue will yield a mild flavor, whereas Stilton or Gorgonzola will create a more pungent tartlet.

Savory Tartlet Dough (recipe follows)

8 oz cream cheese

8 oz blue cheese

2 large eggs

½ cup heavy cream

¼ cup sour cream

1 Tbsp minced chives

1 Tbsp minced flat-leaf parsley

2 tsp minced thyme

1 tsp minced shallots

½ tsp salt

¼ tsp ground white pepper

1. Roll out the dough and use it to line five 4-in tart pans. Place the tart pans on a sheet pan and blind bake in a pre-heated 350°F oven for 10 minutes.

2. Combine the cheeses in a mixing bowl and beat until smooth. Beat in the eggs 1 at a time, beating well after each addition and scraping down the bowl often. Add the cream, sour cream, herbs, shallots, salt, and pepper and beat until smooth.

3. Pour the mixture into the prepared crusts and bake at 300°F until a knife comes out clean when inserted in the center of the tart, about 10 minutes.

4. Let the tarts rest at least 10 minutes before serving. They can be served warm or at room temperature.

SAVORY TARTLET DOUGH

MAKES 1 POUND OF DOUGH

THIS DOUGH can be used to make any type of tart (large or small) that is to be filled with a savory filling. Line tartlet molds and pre-bake them. Fill them with any rillettes or confit mixture and add an appropriate garnish of finely chopped herbs for a quick and delicious hors d'oeuvre.

4 cups bread flour

2 tsp baking powder

1 tsp salt

1 tsp sugar

½ cup butter, cold, cut into cubes

1 egg

2 tsp cider vinegar

1 cup whole milk

1. Combine all of the dry ingredients in a bowl and mix together well.

2. Using your fingertips, rub the butter into the dry ingredients until the mixture appears crumbly and looks like coarse meal.

3. Mix the wet ingredients into the dough until fully incorporated. Knead the dough until smooth and not sticky.

4. Shape the dough into a disk, wrap tightly in plastic wrap, and refrigerate for at least 1 hour before rolling out.

AT LEFT: Blue Cheese Tartlets

Savory Roquefort Cheesecake

MAKES 24 SERVINGS

SERVE THIS beautiful cake sliced into wedges and serve with a drizzle of well-aged balsamic vinegar. Use a warm knife to cut the cake and clean the blade off after every slice so the pieces will be smooth. For bite-size hors d'oeuvre, bake the cake in a parchment-lined 9 × 13-inch baking pan. Cut into 1-inch cubes using a sharp, clean, warm knife and arrange on a platter with toothpicks or skewers.

⅓ cup dry bread crumbs

2 Tbsp butter

2 cups walnuts, toasted and finely chopped

1 lb 4 oz cream cheese

2¼ oz Roquefort cheese

4 large eggs

3 shallots

¼ cup heavy cream

2 Tbsp all-purpose flour

2 tsp chopped dill

1. Brown the bread crumbs in the butter in a sauté pan; add the toasted walnuts and sauté until fragrant. Cool the crumb mixture and press it onto the bottom and sides of a 9-in springform pan.

2. Line the pan with a 3-in paper collar.

3. In a food processor, blend the cheeses until smooth. Add the eggs, shallots, cream, and flour. Blend in the dill and pour into the prepared pan.

4. Bake the cake in a water bath in a preheated 300°F oven until set, about 30 minutes.

5. Cool cake completely. Cover with plastic wrap and refrigerate overnight before unmolding. Cut the cake into 24 equal slices prior to serving.

Mozzarella Cheese

MAKES 2 LB

*I*T'S ACTUALLY easy and also a good bit of fun to make fresh mozzarella cheese. The hardest part is finding the curds to make it with, but today even if one of your local markets doesn't carry them, you can surely find them on the Internet.

¾ cup salt

1 gal water

2 lb cheese curd, cut into ½-in cubes

1. Add the salt to the water in a stockpot and bring to 160°F. Remove the pot from the heat.

2. Put the cheese curd in a colander and lower it into the hot water; the curds must be completely submerged.

3. Work the curd with wooden spoons, stretching it until it becomes a smooth but stringy mass. Maintain the water temperature at a constant 160°F during this process.

4. Remove the cheese from the water and continue stretching it on a clean work surface until the curd is smooth, being careful not to overwork it or the cheese will become tough.

5. Add the cheese to a bowl of ice water and "work" it until it is pliable enough to be shaped. Tear off 4-oz pieces of the cheese and shape into balls.

STORAGE Wrap the balls in plastic wrap, twisting the ends of the plastic wrap together to secure them, or store the cheese balls in a container with enough brine to cover. Store the cheese in the refrigerator up to 5 days.

Marinated Bocconcini

MAKES 2 LB

SUBSTITUTE DIFFERENT vinegars or herbs to vary the taste. Use red wine vinegar or balsamic vinegar and any number of herbs including oregano, thyme, or rosemary. Chop the herbs if they are fresh to release their flavors.

2 lb bocconcini (mozzarella balls that are about 1-in diameter)

3 Tbsp olive oil

1 Tbsp sherry vinegar

¼ cup basil chiffonade

½ tsp red pepper flakes

Combine all the ingredients in a bowl and toss to coat. Cover and marinate in the refrigerator overnight.

MOZZARELLA

Mozzarella is a soft, mild cheese that is extremely versatile. For a delicious salad, layer slices of mozzarella, fresh tomatoes, and basil and top with extra-virgin olive oil, aged balsamic vinegar, cracked black pepper, and sea salt. A smaller variation of this salad can be made on garlic crostinis for a simple canapé. As well, miniature bruschetta make a recognizable hors d'oeuvre and can be topped with fresh mozzarella for a slight variation.

AT LEFT: Marinated Bocconcini (front) and Mozzarella Roulade with Prosciutto (back, page 170)

Mozzarella Roulade with Prosciutto

*S*PREAD THE mozzarella evenly so that it rolls up in a balanced coil. When the roulade is sliced, the beautiful colors and dramatic layers will surely impress guests.

2 qt water

⅓ cup salt

3 cups cheese curd, cut into 1-in cubes

½ tsp ground black pepper

20 basil leaves

5 oz thinly sliced prosciutto

GARNISH

basil leaves

small tomato wedges

1. Combine the water and salt in a large saucepan or Dutch oven and bring to 170°F.

2. Place the cheese curds in a colander and submerge in the hot water. Press and "work" the cheese with the back of a spoon until it becomes one mass and takes on some stringiness.

3. Remove the cheese from the water and knead lightly with the spoon while it is still in the colander, until the mass becomes smooth. Don't overwork, as that will toughen the mozzarella, and you will need to have it pliant enough to press out into a rectangle.

4. Lay a sheet of plastic wrap on the work surface, place the mozzarella on top, and spread it by hand into a ⅛-in-thick rectangle.

5. Sprinkle the pepper evenly over the warm cheese; cover with the basil leaves and a thin layer of sliced prosciutto.

6. Using the plastic wrap to help guide the cheese, roll up like a jelly roll into a tight roulade. Wrap with plastic wrap and secure the ends tightly with string. Use your hands to shape the roulade into an even cylinder, then wrap again with aluminum foil so that it holds its shape. Refrigerate for at least 1 hour.

7. To serve, cut the roulade crosswise into ¾-in slices and place on a plate. Garnish with basil and tomatoes.

NOTE: You can make this in 2 batches, forming 2 roulades, if you find it difficult to work with 1 lb of curds.

AT RIGHT: *When rolling the roulade, use plastic wrap in much the same fashion as a sushi mat to ensure that the roll is tight and even.*

Lemon Cheese

MAKES 12 SERVINGS

*T*HIS TANGY, creamy fresh cheese and its two variations make simple but delicious hors d'oeuvre eaten as they are. They are perfect as an antipasto or serve as a simple dessert with a drizzle of chestnut honey.

1 gal milk

1 qt heavy cream

1¼ cups lemon juice, strained and chilled

2 tsp salt

½ tsp grated lemon zest

1. Combine the milk and cream in a large nonreactive stockpot over simmering water to exactly 100°F (not higher).

2. Remove the stockpot from the heat and add the lemon juice to the milk mixture. Stir very gently and briefly until the milk and cream mixture starts to curdle or thicken. Let stand at room temperature for 3 to 4 hours.

3. Line a colander with cheesecloth and place in a large bowl or place a muslin bag in a bowl. Pour the curd mixture into the cheesecloth or muslin and drain over another bowl. Place the colander and bowl or suspend the bag over the bowl in the refrigerator and drain the curd for 8 to 12 hours.

4. Transfer the cheese to a bowl and "work" in the salt and lemon zest with wooden spoons. Be careful not to overwork the cheese.

5. Press the cheese into a mold set in a shallow bowl, top with a weight, cover, and refrigerate overnight. The cheese is now ready to unmold and serve.

NOTE: Unmold the cheese into a shallow bowl and cover with plastic wrap. Store in the refrigerator up to 4 days.

VARIATIONS

PEPPERED LEMON CHEESE: Add 2 tsp coarse ground black pepper to the cheese with the lemon zest.

DRIED FRUIT AND HAZELNUT CHEESE: Replace the lemon zest with ½ cup each of toasted hazelnuts and dried fruit.

Herbed Yogurt Cheese

YOGURT CHEESE can be made from low-fat or nonfat yogurt with tasty results. It makes a fabulous dip for crackers or vegetables, or use it as a spread on tea sandwiches, topped with sprouts, microgreens, or smoked fish.

2 qt plain yogurt

2½ tsp coarse ground black pepper

1 tsp salt

1 Tbsp chopped oregano

2 tsp chopped thyme

2 small jalapeños, split

2 bay leaves

2 cups extra-virgin olive oil

1. Mix the yogurt, pepper, and salt in a large bowl. Line a colander with cheesecloth and place in a large bowl or place a muslin bag in a bowl. Pour the yogurt mixture into the cheesecloth or muslin and drain over another bowl. Place the colander and bowl or suspend the bag over the bowl in the refrigerator and drain the curd for 3 days.

2. Divide the cheese into 2-oz portions and place on parchment-lined sheet pans. Cover the cheeses with plastic wrap and refrigerate overnight to drain and dry.

3. Combine the remaining ingredients in a shallow bowl and mix well. Put the cheeses in the bowl and spoon some marinade over each. Cover with plastic wrap and marinate in the refrigerator at least 24 hours before serving.

STORAGE: The cheeses can be kept in the marinade, covered with plastic wrap, in the refrigerator up to 4 weeks.

Baked Brie with Caramelized Onions

MAKES 20 SERVINGS

*T*HIS EASY-TO-MAKE appetizer is as rich and decadent as it is hard to stop eating. It is guaranteed to be a crowd-pleaser and is gorgeous to boot. The sweetness of the caramelized onions and the rich, melted cheese creates a memorable appetizer.

2 Tbsp butter

6 cups thinly sliced onions

1½ Tbsp roughly chopped garlic

2 tsp salt plus extra if needed

1 Tbsp minced thyme

½ cup Calvados or brandy

1 tsp ground black pepper plus extra if needed

2-lb Brie cheese wheel in wood box

1. Melt the butter in a very large heavy skillet over medium-high heat. Add the onions; sauté until just tender, 5 to 6 minutes, stirring frequently. Add the garlic and 1 tsp salt, reduce the heat to medium, and cook until the onions are golden, stirring often, 20 to 23 minutes. Add the thyme and sauté until fragrant, about 1 minute. Add ¼ cup Calvados and the remaining salt; stir until almost all the liquid evaporates, about 1 minute. Sauté the onions until they are soft and brown, 6 to 8 minutes. Add the remaining ¼ cup Calvados; stir just until the liquid evaporates, about 1 minute, scraping the bottom to remove the caramelized onion bits from the pan. Season the onions with salt and pepper. Cool to room temperature.

2. Freeze the Brie wheel for 30 minutes before baking to prevent the cheese from oozing over the edge of the box.

3. Unwrap the Brie, reserving the bottom of the wood box. Cut away only the top rind of cheese, leaving the rind on the sides and bottom intact. Return the Brie to the box, rind side down. Place the box on a sheet pan. Top the Brie evenly with the onion mixture. Bake in a preheated 350°F oven until the cheese starts to melt, about 30 minutes.

4. Serve immediately.

NOTE: The onions can be prepared 2 days ahead of serving the Brie. Put cooled onions in a storage container and store in the refrigerator.

AT LEFT: Baked Brie with Caramelized Onions

Chapter Eight

BITE-SIZE DESSERTS

✣

*A*DISPLAY OF BITE-SIZE desserts can be the perfect and dramatic end to any party or the main event of a party on their own. Finish any gathering, from a sit-down dinner to an hors d'oeuvre or cocktail party, with an eye-catching assortment and thoughtfully selected variety to send guests on their way with a sweet taste in their mouths.

SELECTING A MENU OF MINIATURE DESSERTS

Planning a dessert menu should be fun, not a challenge. Keep in mind the season and weather, the time and place, the preparation time, and the preferences of your guests. Here are some considerations for making your sweets stand up to tests other than taste:

- *Select desserts according to the time of year. If it is summer and the heat is raging, a menu of only rich, gooey chocolate delights may not be that appetizing to your guests. Conversely, if it is a cold blustery day, light, airy textures and citrus flavors will not be enticing or satisfying to your guests as would a plate of indulgent chocolate truffles and a glass of red wine.*

- *It's a sad thing to watch a dessert melt before anyone gets to eat it. Chocolate truffles that would be enticing on a cold and blustery day wouldn't last 5 minutes sitting in the sun before they turned into something more closely resembling a mud puddle. For such occasions as an afternoon birthday party by the pool, consider items that can withstand the elements: fruit tartlets, lemon fantasy tartlets, and cookies.*

- *Transporting bite-size desserts is not as big a worry as the weather, because, miniature desserts travel well if packed securely in covered containers.*

- *Be realistic about the amount of preparation time. Consider fewer, easier recipes than many, difficult ones. Take the time necessary to give the attention to each item that it requires. Working too fast can cause mistakes to happen in the kitchen. Careless measuring or sloppy work leads to increasing frustration that might get taken out on co-workers and family, or trickle down into the atmosphere of the event.*

- *Select a variety of items that reflect different flavor profiles. An all-chocolate buffet sounds like heaven to many people, but is not much fun for the guest who is allergic to chocolate or simply doesn't enjoy it. To serve a gaggle of small children, remember that, in general, little ones enjoy simpler flavors and usually NO NUTS, MOM!*

- *Offer a variety of not only flavors, but also textures. Have something smooth and creamy, soft and downy, and crisp and crunchy. Make sure to have something that will entice each and every person attending the party.*

PLANNING YOUR PREPARATION SCHEDULE

When planning a menu, take time to write down a preparation schedule and post it in a visible spot.

When baking in volume, group similar tasks: measure all recipe ingredients on one day, mix all on the second, and assemble and bake on the third day.

Look carefully at the recipes for the things that can be done ahead of time without compromising the flavor or texture of the finished product.

- *Make cookie and tart dough that will keep ahead of time. Wrap them in plastic wrap and refrigerate until ready to bake.*

- *Make cookies that do not easily stale, such as biscotti, ahead of time and store them in airtight containers.*

- *Bake tart shells a day or two ahead of time and store them in airtight containers.*

- *If the temperature and humidity are low, make chocolate desserts, such as truffles and knackerli, a day or two ahead of the party and store them in covered containers.*

Plan with care, and the party will go off without a hitch. Everyone will relax and enjoy themselves.

DESSERT BEVERAGES

Serving the right beverage can complement the flavors in the desserts offered. Some traditional choices include:

COFFEE AND TEA

Consider the old standbys of coffee and tea and offer both caffeinated and decaffeinated versions.

- *If serving a flavored coffee, make sure that it is mellow enough to complement all of the dessert items. Vanilla and cinnamon flavors are usually safe bets. Consider serving a pot of a generic Colombian blend along with one of flavored coffee.*

- *If serving tea, offer at least one herbal in addition to a traditional black or blend that will appeal to all. Some herbal teas that marry well with desserts are peppermint, chamomile, and ginger.*

- *Provide milk, half-and-half, sugar, and honey.*

WINES

A sophisticated palate appreciates the complexities of a thoughtful match of wine with dessert, but some wines are natural partners. It's better to stick with these than ruin an otherwise delightful dessert buffet with a wine with too strong a personality.

- *Sparkling wines, such as Champagne, Prosecco, or Cava, are good choices as their flavors marry well with just about anything. You only need to choose sweet or dry (sec or brut).*

- *Red wines, such as full-bodied Burgundy Merlot, are surprisingly enjoyable with the rich and flavorful tone in dark chocolate.*

- *There are many sweet and fruity wines that are almost exclusively drunk alone or with dessert. A few suggestions are:*

  Ice wine (Eiswein)—Serve with fruit or light desserts.

  Madeira—Serve with milk chocolate or almond or hazelnut tarts.

  Port—Serve with pears or apples or dark-chocolate desserts.

  Sauternes—Serve with fresh fruit tarts or caramel flavors.

  Muscat—Serve with chocolate or fruit desserts.

Honey Tuile Cups

MAKES 48 TUILE CUPS

*T*HE HONEY flavor in this batter comes through beautifully. It is very easy to work with and the tuiles are easy to shape. Once the inside of the tuile is coated with melted chocolate, it can be filled with fruit salad, a mousse, or even a small scoop of ice cream.

5 Tbsp butter, soft

⅔ cup confectioners' sugar, sifted

2 Tbsp honey

1 large egg white

¾ cup all-purpose flour, sifted

1. Cream the butter and sugar in a mixer bowl on medium speed with a paddle attachment until smooth, about 3 minutes. Add the honey and egg white, blending until fully incorporated. Scrape down the bowl.

2. On low speed, mix in the flour. Scrape down the bowl as needed to blend evenly.

3. Draw twelve 2-in circles on 4 pieces of parchment paper. Turn over each piece of parchment onto a sheet pan.

Using an offset spatula, spread ½ tsp of batter evenly within each circle.

4. Bake cookies, 1 sheet at a time, in a preheated 325°F oven until golden brown, about 6 minutes. Remove the cookies from the oven and immediately shape as desired (for "tiles" curl cookies top side up over a rolling pin or fat wooden-spoon handle; for cups, mold cookies top side down into tartlet pans or muffin cups), or leave the cookies flat and cool in the pans on racks. Repeat with the remaining prepared parchment sheets.

STORAGE: The tuiles can be baked a day in advance and stored (unfilled) in an airtight container.

NOTE: The batter can be made up to 2 days ahead of time.

Chocolate Mousse in Tuile Cups

T HIS CHOCOLATE mousse is rich and thick, just the way it should be. The tuile (French for "tile" because they are traditionally shaped like curved roof tiles) cups can be filled with the mousse the day before, if necessary, but it is best to fill and serve them fresh.

24 Honey Tuile Cups (page 180)

2 oz bittersweet chocolate, finely chopped and melted

CHOCOLATE MOUSSE

¾ cup bittersweet chocolate, melted

1½ Tbsp butter

3 large egg yolks

½ cup sugar

1½ tsp water

3 large egg whites

½ cup heavy cream, whipped to soft peaks

1. Brush the inside of the tuiles with the melted 2 oz chocolate and set aside until the chocolate is set, about 10 minutes.

2. Combine the ¾ cup chocolate and the butter and melt over a hot water bath. Set aside and keep warm.

3. Combine the egg yolks, 2 Tbsp sugar, and the water in a heat-safe mixing bowl and whisk over a hot water bath to 145°F for 15 seconds. Remove from the heat and whisk until cool.

4. Combine the egg whites and the remaining sugar in another heat-safe mixing bowl and heat, whisking constantly, for about 15 seconds over a hot water bath to 145°F. Remove from the heat and beat at high speed until stiff peaks form, about 4 minutes. Continue beating until the meringue has completely cooled, 6 to 8 minutes.

5. Using a large rubber spatula, fold the egg whites into the egg yolks.

6. Fold one-third of the egg mixture into the chocolate mixture to lighten it. Fold in the remaining egg mixture.

7. Gently blend about one-third of the whipped cream into the chocolate mixture. Fold in the remaining whipped cream, thoroughly incorporating it.

8. Immediately spoon or pipe about 1 tsp of the mousse using a No. 4 pastry tip into the prepared tuiles. Cover with plastic wrap and refrigerate until completely set.

Raspberry Mousse in Tuile Cups

MAKES 24 TUILE CUPS

THE SWEET-TART flavor of the raspberry mousse is the perfect complement for the chocolate and the honey tuile. If the time of year is right, garnish each with a fresh raspberry and a sprig of mint.

24 Honey Tuile Cups (page 180)

2 oz bittersweet chocolate, finely chopped and melted

RASPBERRY MOUSSE

1 tsp powdered gelatin

5 Tbsp cold water

1 cup seedless raspberry purée (store-bought or homemade)

½ cup heavy cream

1 large egg white

⅓ cup sugar

1. Brush the inside of the tuile cups with the melted 2 oz chocolate and set aside until the chocolate is set, about 10 minutes.

2. Sprinkle the gelatin over the cold water in a small bowl and stir to break up any clumps. Let the gelatin soften in the water for about 3 minutes. Heat the softened gelatin over simmering water or in a microwave on low power until the granules melt and the mixture is clear, about 20 seconds. Set aside.

3. Warm half the raspberry purée in a saucepan until barely simmering. Remove from the heat. Add the melted gelatin to the purée and stir to blend. Add the remaining purée and stir until melted. Pour the mixture into a large mixing bowl and set aside to cool.

4. Whip the heavy cream to medium peaks in a mixing bowl, cover with plastic wrap, and refrigerate until needed.

5. Combine the egg white and sugar in a heat-safe mixing bowl and heat, whisking constantly, for about 15 seconds over a hot water bath to 145°F. Remove from the heat and beat at high speed until stiff peaks form, about 4 minutes. Continue beating until the meringue has completely cooled, 6 to 8 minutes.

6. Gently blend approximately one-third of the meringue into the raspberry purée mixture to lighten it. Fold in the remaining meringue, thoroughly incorporating it. Fold in the reserved whipped cream.

7. Immediately spoon or pipe about 1 tsp of the mousse using a No. 4 pastry tip into the prepared tuiles. Cover and refrigerate until completely set, about 1 hour.

VARIATIONS

RASPBERRY EXTRAVAGANZA: Garnish the mousse-filled tuiles with fresh raspberries, lemon zest, and whipped cream.

CHOCOLATE FIX: Top the mousse-filled tuiles with a rosette of whipped cream and a sprinkle of chocolate shavings.

Rich Short Dough

MAKES 3 LB 4 OZ

*T*HIS DOUGH doesn't have to be weighted down to prebake the tartlet shells. This helps when you are working with miniature pastries.

2 cups (4 sticks) butter, soft

1¾ cups confectioners' sugar, sifted

½ tsp vanilla extract

1 Tbsp grated lemon zest

14 large egg yolks

6 cups cake flour, sifted

1. In a mixer fitted with a paddle attachment, combine the butter, sugar, vanilla extract, and lemon zest on medium speed, scraping down the bowl as needed, until the mixture is smooth and light in color, 3 to 4 minutes.

2. Add the egg yolks gradually, scraping down the bowl and blending until smooth after each addition. Add the flour all at once and mix on low speed just until blended.

3. Turn the dough out onto a lightly floured work surface. Divide the dough into recipe-ready amounts as desired. Wrap each portion tightly in plastic wrap and refrigerate for at least 1 hour before rolling.

STORAGE: The dough can be wrapped in plastic wrap and refrigerated up to 1 week or frozen for later use.

TIPS FOR MAKING TENDER SHORT DOUGH

Two of the most important components to making good short dough are the type of flour used in the recipe and the process of mixing the dough. Cake flour is the first choice for making short dough. Because of its relatively high starch content, cake flour absorbs a lot of moisture and has to be worked much more to become tough. In mixing short dough it is important at every stage not to overmix the dough. Blend the butter and sugar at a low speed just to a smooth paste. If you mix too vigorously, you may incorporate too much air, which would adversely affect the crumb of the finished dough. Blend in the eggs at low speed as well. Add the flour all at once and mix only until just combined to create the tenderest crust. After mixing, refrigerate the dough so that it becomes firm and will not become overworked when rolled.

Lemon Meringue Tartlets

MAKES 24 TARTLETS

*T*HESE DARLINGS of the dessert table are perfect two-bite sweets. They are very easy to make, and the signature meringue topping doesn't have to be piped on—just spoon it.

12 oz Rich Short Dough (page 183)

LEMON CURD

½ cup (1 stick) butter, cubed, plus extra for greasing tartlet pans

⅔ cup sugar

½ cup lemon juice

1 Tbsp grated lemon zest

7 large egg yolks

MERINGUE

2 large egg whites

⅔ cup sugar

1. For the tartlet shells: Grease twenty-four 2-in tartlet pans, place on a sheet pan, and set aside. Roll out the dough on the work surface to a ⅛-in thickness and cut out twenty-four 2¼-in rounds using a cookie cutter. Line the tart pans with the dough rounds. Prick the dough with a fork and refrigerate until the dough is firm, about 10 minutes.

2. Bake the tartlet shells in a preheated 350°F oven until very light golden brown, 10 to 12 minutes. Cool the tart shells completely in the pans, remove, and place on a sheet pan.

3. For the lemon curd, combine half the butter, half the sugar, and the lemon juice and zest in a small saucepan and bring to a boil over medium heat, stirring gently to dissolve the sugar, about 3 minutes.

4. Meanwhile, blend the egg yolks with the remaining sugar in a medium heat-safe bowl. Temper by gradually adding about one-third of the lemon juice mixture, whisking constantly. Return the tempered egg mixture to the saucepan. Continue cooking, whisking constantly, until the mixture thickens and comes to a simmer, 2 to 3 minutes.

5. Stir in the remaining butter.

6. Strain the curd into a shallow container or bowl. Cool the curd over an ice bath, stirring constantly, until it reaches room temperature.

7. Spoon or pipe 2 tsp of lemon curd into each tartlet shell. (The curd should just come to the top of the shell without overflowing.) Cover the tartlets with plastic wrap and refrigerate until needed.

8. For the meringue, place the egg whites in the bowl of an electric mixer. Beat them on high speed until frothy and gradually beat in the sugar. Beat the meringue on high speed until medium peaks form, about 8 minutes. Pipe or dollop the meringue on top of the tartlets and brown the tops of the tartlets using a torch or under the broiler. Serve immediately.

AT LEFT: Lemon Meringue Tartlets

Cranberry Pecan Tartlets

*T*HE BUTTERY, rich pastry, pecans, and brown sugar together with the cranberries make the perfect marriage of flavors. To add an extra dimension, drizzle the tops of the cooled tartlets with melted chocolate or top with lightly sweetened whipped cream.

12 oz Rich Short Dough (page 183)

¼ cup butter

½ cup light corn syrup

⅓ cup packed light brown sugar

1 large egg

¾ tsp vanilla extract

½ cup pecans, chopped

½ cup pecan halves

12 cranberries, halved

1. For the tartlet shells: Grease twenty-four 2-in tartlet pans, place on a sheet pan, and set aside. Roll out the dough on the work surface to a ⅛-in thickness and cut out twenty-four 2¼-in rounds using a cookie cutter. Line the tart pans with the dough rounds. Prick the dough with a fork and refrigerate until the dough is firm, about 10 minutes.

2. Bake the tartlet shells in a preheated 350°F oven until very light golden brown, 10 to 12 minutes. Cool the tart shells completely in the pans, remove, and place on a sheet pan.

3. Combine the butter, corn syrup, and sugar in a saucepan and bring to a simmer over medium heat, stirring, until the sugar has dissolved, about 3 minutes. Remove from the heat.

4. Whisk the egg in a medium bowl until fluffy. Blend in the sugar mixture. Blend in the vanilla extract.

5. Place 1 tsp of chopped pecans in each tartlet shell. Pour 1½ tsp of filling into each shell over the chopped pecans. Arrange the pecan halves and halved cranberries on top of the filling.

6. Bake tartlets in a preheated 350°F oven until the filling is set, 5 to 7 minutes. Cool completely and serve, or cover and refrigerate until serving.

Lemon Fantasy Tartlets

*T*HESE MINIATURE "lemon bars in a tart shell" hold well overnight in the refrigerator. Add the garnish just before serving to be sure the cream and raspberries look and taste their best.

12 oz Rich Short Dough (page 183)

2 large eggs

½ cup sugar

5 Tbsp heavy cream

½ tsp grated lemon zest

¼ cup lemon juice

GARNISH

¼ cup heavy cream, whipped to soft peaks

6 raspberries, quartered just before using

1. For the tartlet shells: Grease twenty-four 2-in tartlet pans, place on a sheet pan, and set aside. Roll out the dough on the work surface to a ⅛-in thickness and cut out twenty-four 2¼-in rounds using a cookie cutter. Line the tart pans with the dough rounds. Prick the surface of the dough with a fork and refrigerate until the dough is firm, about 10 minutes.

2. Bake the tartlet shells in a preheated 350°F oven until very light golden brown, 10 to 12 minutes. Cool the tart shells completely in the pans, remove, and place on a sheet pan.

3. Combine the eggs and sugar in a bowl and whisk until blended.

4. In another bowl, beat the cream to soft peaks.

5. Add the lemon zest and juice to the egg mixture. Fold in the whipped cream.

6. Spoon about 1½ tsp of filling into each tart shell. Bake in a preheated 350°F oven until the filling is very soft but set, 6 to 8 minutes. Cool completely.

7. Cover the tartlets with plastic wrap and refrigerate overnight, or until fully set. Garnish each with whipped cream and raspberry quarters or as desired.

Bittersweet Chocolate-Orange Tartlets

MAKES 24 TARTLETS

*A*LTHOUGH EVERYONE will want to, no one can eat more than one of these rich, dark chocolate treats. Serve them with a dollop of lightly sweetened whipped cream, or a piece of an orange segment on top to brighten the flavor.

12 oz Rich Tart Dough (page 183)

¾ cup heavy cream

3 Tbsp sugar

1 Tbsp grated orange zest

6 large egg yolks

3 oz bittersweet chocolate, finely chopped, melted

2 Tbsp orange-flavored liqueur

1. For the tartlet shells: Grease twenty-four 2-in tartlet pans, place on a sheet pan, and set aside. Roll out the dough on the work surface to a ⅛-in thickness and cut out twenty-four 2¼-in rounds using a cookie cutter. Line the tart pans with the dough rounds. Prick the dough with a fork and refrigerate until the dough is firm, about 10 minutes.

2. Bake the tartlet shells in a preheated 350°F oven until very light golden brown, 10 to 12 minutes. Cool the tart shells completely in the pans, remove, and place on a sheet pan.

3. Combine the cream, 2 Tbsp sugar, and the orange zest in a saucepan and bring to a boil. Remove from the heat, cover, and steep 5 minutes.

4. Blend the egg yolks with the remaining sugar in a medium bowl. While whisking constantly, gradually add about one-third of the hot cream mixture into the yolks. Blend in the remaining hot cream.

5. Add the chocolate and liqueur to the orange custard mixture, blending well. Strain the custard into a small bowl.

6. Divide the filling evenly among the tartlet shells, filling them to ⅛ in from the top.

7. Bake the tartlets a preheated 325°F oven until the custard is soft but set, about 10 minutes. Cool to room temperature.

8. Serve the tartlets chilled or at room temperature.

Almond and Pine Nut Tartlets

MAKES 24 TARTLETS

*T*HESE CLASSIC Italian flavors make a delicately flavored, but memorable impression. The confectioners' sugar should be applied just before serving so that it is not dissolved by the moisture in the filling and will still be visible.

12 oz Rich Short Dough (page 183)

3 large eggs

6 oz almond paste

1 Tbsp sugar

1 tsp vanilla extract

¼ cup plus 2 Tbsp all-purpose flour

½ cup pine nuts

confectioners' sugar for dusting the tartlets

1. For the tartlet shells: Grease twenty-four 2-in tartlet pans, place on a sheet pan, and set aside. Roll out the dough on the work surface to a ⅛-in thickness and cut out twenty-four 2¼-in rounds using a cookie cutter. Line the tart pans with the dough rounds.

2. Combine 1 egg, the almond paste, and sugar in a bowl and whisk until smooth. Add the remaining eggs one at a time, mixing until fully incorporated after each addition. Blend in the vanilla. Add the flour and mix just until incorporated.

3. Spoon the filling into each of the lined tartlet molds, dividing equally, and sprinkle a few pine nuts on top of each.

4. Bake the tartlets in a preheated 350°F oven until the filling is set, about 15 minutes.

5. Cool the tartlets completely and dust with confectioners' sugar in a fine sieve.

Miniature Chocolate Éclairs

MAKES 32 PASTRIES

ALTHOUGH A little challenging to make, these extra-delicious and very cute pastries are worth the effort. Make the shells a day or two ahead of time if you are pressed for time.

¼ recipe Pâte à Choux (page 15)

1 large egg

1 Tbsp milk

¾ cup Diplomat Cream (page 192)

1 cup heavy cream, whipped to soft peaks

1½ cups Hard Ganache (recipe follows)

1. Fold a half sheet pan size piece of parchment paper in half lengthwise and fold it in half again. Fold the paper crosswise in half, then in half, then in half again. Unfold the paper. There should be 32 "boxes" on the parchment paper. These will act as a guide for the length of the éclairs.

2. Pipe 4 dots of pâte à choux in the corners of the sheet pan and line the pan with the parchment paper guide, using the pâte à choux to glue the parchment paper to the pan.

3. Pipe the pâte à choux into cylinders 2½ in long on the parchment-lined pan, using a No. 6 plain piping tip. Combine the egg and milk in a cup to make an egg wash and lightly brush the top of each pastry.

4. Bake the pastries in a preheated 360°F oven until the cracks formed in the pastries are no longer yellow, about 50 minutes.

5. Pierce the bottom of the éclairs using a skewer or similar instrument to make a ⅛- to ³/₁₆-in-diameter hole. Let pastries cool to room temperature.

6. Fill the éclairs with diplomat cream using a No. 1 plain piping tip.

7. Top the filled éclairs with the chocolate ganache either by dipping or by coating them using the back of a spoon.

HARD GANACHE

MAKES 1 LB

THIS TYPE of ganache can be used for glazing cakes or pastries, or fully chilled it can be rolled into balls to make chocolate truffles. The cream can be heated and infused with any flavoring, from fresh grated ginger to lemon to a favorite tea, before adding the chocolate.

1 lb bittersweet chocolate, finely chopped

1 cup heavy cream

1. Place the chopped chocolate in a bowl.

2. Heat the cream in a saucepan over medium heat, just to a boil.

3. Pour the cream over the chocolate and let stand for about 3 minutes. Gently stir with a wooden spoon until the chocolate is fully melted and the mixture is completely smooth.

4. Use as a glaze immediately, or refrigerate for later use.

AT LEFT: When finishing éclairs with ganache, set up a station that flows from left to right: unfinished éclairs on your left, glazed in the middle, and finished éclairs on your right.

DIPLOMAT CREAM

MAKES 3 CUPS

THIS CREAM can be used as a filling for a number of pastries. Use it to fill tartlet shells and then simply top with fresh berries or Clementine segments.

1 cup heavy cream

¾ tsp powdered gelatin

2 Tbsp cold water

1 cup Pastry Cream (recipe follows), warm

1. Prepare and assemble the desired pastries, containers, or molds that are to be used with the cream before beginning preparation.

2. Whip the heavy cream in a bowl to soft peaks. Cover with plastic wrap and refrigerate.

3. Sprinkle the gelatin over the cold water in a small bowl and stir to break up any clumps. Let the gelatin soften in the water for about 3 minutes. Heat the softened gelatin over simmering water or in a microwave on low power until the granules melt and the mixture is clear, about 20 seconds.

4. Blend the melted gelatin into the freshly prepared and still-warm pastry cream. Strain, then cool over an ice water bath to 75°F.

5. Gently blend about one-third of the reserved whipped cream into the pastry cream mixture. Fold in the remaining whipped cream until thoroughly blended.

6. Immediately pipe into prepared pastries or containers. Cover and refrigerate until completely set.

PASTRY CREAM

MAKES ABOUT 2 CUPS

A GOOD pastry cream is a staple of any baker's repertoire. Be creative with its flavoring and uses, even using a favorite fruit juice to replace some or all of the milk—just adjust the amount of sugar to compensate for the sweetness of the juice.

¼ cup cornstarch

¾ cup sugar

2 cups whole milk

4 large egg yolks, lightly beaten

pinch of salt

2 tsp vanilla extract

2 Tbsp unsalted butter

1. Combine the cornstarch with ¼ cup sugar in a mixing bowl and stir in ½ cup milk. Blend the yolks into the cornstarch mixture, stirring with a wooden spoon until completely smooth.

2. Prepare an ice bath. Combine the remaining 1½ cups milk with the remaining ½ cup sugar and the salt in a nonreactive saucepan over medium heat and bring to a boil. Remove the pan from the heat.

3. Temper the egg mixture by gradually adding about one-third of the hot milk mixture, while whisking constantly. Add the remaining milk mixture to the eggs. Return the mixture to the saucepan and continue cooking over medium heat, vigorously stirring with a whisk, until the mixture comes to a boil and the whisk leaves a trail in the pastry cream, about 7 minutes. As soon as the cream reaches this stage, remove the pan from the heat and stir in the vanilla extract and butter. Transfer the pan to the ice bath. Stir occasionally until the pastry cream is cool, about 30 minutes.

4. Transfer the pastry cream to a storage container with a lid. Refrigerate until needed, up to 3 days.

Cream Puffs

RATHER THAN serving as a finger-food dessert, serve these pastries on a plate, so they can be savored using a fork. Heat up some chocolate sauce for the final flourish to a sit-down affair.

¼ recipe Pâte à Choux (page 15)

1 large egg

1 Tbsp milk

⅓ cup sliced almonds

⅔ cup Pastry Cream (page 192)

CHANTILLY CREAM

1 cup heavy cream, whipped

2 Tbsp confectioners' sugar plus extra for dusting the pastries

1. Pipe the pâte à choux into 1-in-diameter balls onto parchment-lined sheet pans using a No. 6 plain piping tip. Combine the egg and milk in a cup to make an egg wash and lightly brush the top of each ball.

2. Stick several almond slices into the top of each ball so they protrude from the tops.

3. Bake in a preheated 360°F oven until the cracks formed in the pastries are no longer yellow, about 35 minutes. Cool to room temperature. Slice the tops off each of the baked pastries.

4. Pipe about 1 tsp of pastry cream into the pastry bases using a No. 4 plain pastry tip, without overfilling them. There will be some pastry cream left over.

5. For the Chantilly cream: Beat the heavy cream and 2 Tbsp confectioners' sugar together in a bowl to soft peaks. Pipe about ½ Tbsp of Chantilly cream on top of the pastry cream using a No. 4 star pastry tip, being careful not to overfill them. There will be a little Chantilly cream left over.

6. Place the tops of the pastries on the whipped cream, and lightly dust with confectioners' sugar.

VARIATION

BERRY FILLING: Place a ¼-in-thick strawberry slice or 2 blueberries or ¼ oz of other fruit on top of the pastry cream and then pipe the Chantilly cream onto the fruit.

Knackerli

*T*HE COLORS and shapes of the fruits and nuts make a beautiful addition to any buffet table, and the nuts and fruit are delicious with the chocolate.

1 cup dark, milk, or white chocolate morsels

24 pistachios, peeled

24 dried cherries or cranberries

6 dried apricots, quartered

24 slivered almonds, toasted

1. Melt the chocolate over a double boiler.

2. Spoon the chocolate or fill a parchment cone with the chocolate and pipe 1-in disks (1 tsp per disk) onto a parchment-lined sheet pan.

3. Arrange 1 pistachio, 1 dried cherry or cranberry, 1 piece of dried apricot, and 1 piece of slivered almond onto each disk of chocolate.

4. Let the chocolate fully set before removing the disks from the parchment paper.

NOTES: The chocolate can be piped in larger or smaller disks, if desired. Any type of nuts or dried fruit can be substituted for the pistachios, dried cranberries, and apricots.

When making knackerli, it is important to remember that the size of the nuts and dried fruits corresponds to the size of the chocolate disk and that the colors and flavors complement each other.

AT LEFT: When preparing knackerli, work in small batches so that the chocolate disks don't set before you've had a chance to garnish them.

Coffee Truffles

*E*ASY TO make and a guaranteed crowd-pleaser, these confections can be garnished and refrigerated overnight. Use any nut for garnish instead of the hazelnuts.

1 cup finely chopped dark chocolate

1 Tbsp instant espresso powder

1 Tbsp boiling water

6 Tbsp heavy cream

1 Tbsp corn syrup

½ cup unsweetened cocoa powder, sifted

¾ cup shelled hazelnuts, toasted, skinned, and chopped

1. Place the chocolate in a heat-safe bowl.
2. Blend the espresso and water in a small saucepan to make a paste. Add the heavy cream and corn syrup, whisk until blended, and bring to a simmer. Pour the mixture over the chopped chocolate and stir until the chocolate melts and the mixture is smooth.
3. Pour the ganache into a shallow bowl, cover, and refrigerate until firm, overnight.
4. Using a melon baller, scoop ¾-in balls (1 tsp each) onto a parchment-lined sheet pan. Roll the truffles into balls.
5. Dust some of the truffles in cocoa powder and roll the remaining truffles in the chopped nuts.
6. Cover and refrigerate the truffles until needed.

AT RIGHT: When shaping and finishing truffles, work with the mixture at room temperature so that the chocolate will shape easily in your hands.

Dragéed Macadamia Nuts

MAKES 2 LB

THIS MIGHT be the best candy ever invented. The macadamia nuts are exceptionally decadent and delicious coated in caramel and chocolate.

¾ cup sugar

3 Tbsp water

1 lb raw macadamia nuts

1 Tbsp butter

1½ cups dark chocolate morsels, melted

2 Tbsp unsweetened cocoa powder

1. Combine the sugar and water in a wide, large, heavy saucepan and stir to moisten all the sugar. Cook over medium-high heat, stirring constantly until the syrup comes to a boil, about 2 minutes.

2. When the syrup comes to a boil, stop stirring and skim the surface of the syrup to remove any scum that has formed.

3. Cook the syrup, occasionally washing down the side of the pan using a pastry brush and water, to the long thread stage (215° to 230°F), about 1 minute. Remove from the heat.

4. Add the nuts and stir until the sugar crystallizes, about 2 minutes.

5. Return the pan to medium heat and stir constantly until the sugar melts and caramelizes onto the nuts, about 10 minutes.

6. Add the butter and stir in quickly.

7. Pour the mixture onto a marble slab and separate the nuts immediately with a fork. Let the candy cool on the slab to room temperature, about 30 minutes.

8. Cool the candy 3 minutes in the freezer.

9. Add ½ cup chocolate and stir until the chocolate sets up so the nuts don't stick together. Repeat with another ½ cup of chocolate.

10. Add the last ½ cup of chocolate and stir until it is almost set up. Add the cocoa powder and stir to coat.

11. Place the candy in a sieve and shake off any excess cocoa powder.

NOTE: Most any other nut can be substituted for macadamia nuts. Nuts should not be toasted as they roast during the caramelization of the sugar.

Miniature Chocolate Chunk Cookies

MAKES 45 COOKIES

DEPENDING ON how long you bake these cookies, you can make them either crisp and crunchy, or bake them for a slightly shorter time for a moist and chewy version.

3½ cups all-purpose flour

1 tsp salt

2 tsp baking powder

1½ cups (3 sticks) butter

1 cup sugar

⅔ cup packed light brown sugar

3 large eggs

2 tsp vanilla extract

2¾ cups semisweet chocolate pieces

1. Line sheet pans with parchment paper.

2. Sift together the flour, salt, and baking powder into a large mixing bowl.

3. In a mixer fitted with a paddle attachment, cream the butter and sugars on medium speed, scraping down the bowl as needed, until the mixture is smooth and light in color, about 5 minutes.

4. Combine the eggs and the vanilla extract in a bowl and whisk until blended. Add the egg mixture to the butter-sugar mixture in 3 additions, mixing until fully incorporated after each addition and scraping down the bowl as necessary.

5. Add the dry ingredients on low speed, mixing until just incorporated. Blend in the chocolate pieces.

6. Drop 1 Tbsp of the dough onto the lined pans, leaving 1½ in between each cookie.

7. Bake in a preheated 375°F oven until golden brown, 10 to 15 minutes for a crisp cookie.

Raspberry Rugalach

MAKES 72 COOKIES

*F*ILL THESE as the recipe specifies, or use your favorite jam and nuts, and throw in a few chocolate morsels, too. Be creative and use spices that suit your taste, or the season, or occasion.

4 cups bread flour

1 cup all-purpose flour

1 tsp salt

3 cups (6 sticks) butter

1 lb 4 oz cream cheese

1 cup seedless raspberry jam

4 cups chopped pecans

1 cup milk

½ cup cinnamon sugar (1 tsp cinnamon mixed with ½ cup sugar)

1. Line sheet pans with parchment paper.

2. Sift together the flours and salt into a bowl.

3. In a mixer fitted with a paddle attachment, mix the butter and cream cheese together on medium speed until smooth, about 5 minutes. On low speed, mix in the sifted dry ingredients until just combined, scraping down the bowl as necessary to blend evenly.

4. Turn the dough onto a work surface. Roll the dough into a 14 × 10-in rectangle, ½ in thick. Administer one "three fold" by visually dividing the rectangle into thirds and folding one third over the center third and then folding over the remaining third. Divide the dough into 4 equal portions, wrap each tightly in plastic wrap, and refrigerate overnight or until cool enough to roll out.

5. Working with 1 piece of dough at a time, roll out the dough to an 18 × 12-in rectangle, ⅛ in thick.

6. Spread ¼ cup jam evenly over the surface and evenly sprinkle with 1 cup chopped pecans. Beginning with one 18-in side, roll into a log. (The log will stretch to approximately 24 in long while rolling.) Brush the log with milk and sprinkle with 2 Tbsp cinnamon sugar. Cut the log into ¾-in-wide sections. Repeat with the remaining dough.

7. Bake the rugalach in a preheated 375°F oven until golden brown, about 20 minutes. Remove them to wire racks to cool.

AT LEFT, BACK TO FRONT: Raspberry Rugalach, Pecan Diamonds (page 204), Miniature Almond-Anise Biscotti (page 202), Miniature Chocolate Chunk Cookies (page 199), Miniature Almond-Anise Biscotti, Raspberry Rugalach

Miniature Almond-Anise Biscotti

MAKES 64 BISCOTTI

*T*HESE CLASSIC biscotti never lose their appeal. Serve them with coffee, espresso, tea, or a fine bottle of Vin Santo wine. To make them richer, mix in chocolate chips with the almonds, or dip one end of each cookie in chocolate after they are baked and cooled.

2 cups bread flour

1 tsp baking powder

3 large eggs

¾ cup sugar

1 tsp anise extract

¼ tsp salt

1⅓ cups whole almonds

2 Tbsp anise seeds

1. Line sheet pans with parchment paper.

2. Sift together the bread flour and baking powder into a large mixing bowl.

3. In a mixer fitted with a paddle attachment, beat the eggs, sugar, anise extract, and salt on high speed until thick and light in color, about 5 minutes. Mix in the flour mixture on low speed, just until incorporated. Using a rubber spatula, fold in the almonds and anise seeds.

4. Form the dough into four 8-in-long strips on the lined sheet pans.

5. Bake in a preheated 300°F oven until light golden brown, about 1 hour. Remove the pan from the oven and cool for 10 minutes. Lower the oven temperature to 275°F.

6. Using a serrated knife, cut each strip crosswise into ½-in-thick slices. Place the biscotti cut side down on sheet pans and bake until golden brown, 20 minutes, turning the biscotti halfway through the baking time. Transfer to wire racks to cool completely.

Orange Biscotti

*D*IP ONE of the ends of these biscotti in melted dark chocolate after they have cooled and set aside until the chocolate sets. The classic orange-chocolate combination is sure to please all.

2 cups bread flour

1 tsp baking powder

3 large eggs

¾ cup sugar

⅓ cup finely grated orange zest

1 tsp vanilla extract

¼ tsp almond extract

¼ tsp salt

2 cups slivered almonds

1. Line sheet pans with parchment paper.

2. Sift together the bread flour and baking powder into a large mixing bowl.

3. In a mixer fitted with a paddle attachment, beat the eggs, sugar, orange zest, vanilla and almond extracts, and salt on high speed until thick and light in color, about 5 minutes. Mix in the dry ingredients on low speed, just until incorporated. Using a rubber spatula, fold in the slivered almonds.

4. Form the dough into four 12-in-long strips on the lined sheet pans.

5. Bake in a preheated 300°F oven until light golden brown, about 1 hour. Remove the pan from the oven and cool for 10 minutes. Lower the oven temperature to 275°F.

6. Using a serrated knife, cut each strip crosswise into ½-in-thick slices. Place the biscotti cut side down on the sheet pans and bake until golden brown, 20 minutes, turning the biscotti halfway through the baking time. Transfer to wire racks to cool completely.

Pecan Diamonds

MAKES 120 DIAMONDS

*T*HESE RICH and tasty treats can be made even more decadent by drizzling with melted bittersweet chocolate. If making them for a holiday, brighten the flavors and make them more colorful by adding some dried, sweetened cranberries to the pecan mixture before baking.

1 doubled recipe Tart Dough (page 205)

all-purpose flour for rolling dough

2 cups (4 sticks) unsalted butter, diced

2 cups firmly packed light brown sugar

½ cup sugar

1 cup honey

½ cup heavy cream

9 cups whole shelled pecans

1. Line a 17¼ × 11½ × 1-in jelly-roll pan with parchment paper. Roll the tart dough on a lightly floured surface into a ⅛-in-thick rectangle just slightly larger than the dimensions of the pan. Transfer the dough to the pan and gently press it to the sides and bottom. Prick the dough in several places with the tines of a fork. Line the dough with parchment paper and weight with dry beans or rice. Bake until the dough is firm but has no color, 10 to 12 minutes. Remove the weights and let cool completely on a wire rack.

2. Combine the butter, sugars, honey, and cream in a heavy saucepan. Attach a candy thermometer to the side of the pan, making sure that the bulb is submerged but not resting on the bottom of the pan. Cook over medium-high heat, stirring constantly to prevent scorching, until the mixture reaches 240°F. Add the nuts to the boiling mixture, stir until fully incorporated, and then return the mixture to a boil, stirring frequently. Immediately pour into the prepared crust and spread into an even layer.

3. Bake in a preheated 350°F oven until the entire surface of the mixture is evenly covered with bubbles or foam and the crust is brown on the edges, about 40 minutes.

4. Cool completely in the pan on a wire rack. To cut into diamonds, first make straight cuts at 1-in intervals lengthwise. Holding the knife blade so that it intersects the first cuts at a 45-degree angle, make an initial cut as close to the lower left-hand corner of the pecan pastry as possible. Continue to make cuts parallel to the first cut at 1-inch intervals to make regular-shaped pieces, then lift the diamonds from the pan.

Tart Dough

MAKES 1 LB

THIS DELICIOUS, flaky, and crisp dough is equally well suited for any dessert pastry, large or small. Make small prebaked tartlet shells and fill with pastry cream and fresh fruit or chocolate mousse and a sprinkling of shaved chocolate.

½ cup (1 stick) unsalted butter, at room temperature

¼ cup sugar

½ tsp vanilla extract

1 large egg yolk

1½ cups cake flour, plus extra for dusting

1. In a mixer fitted with a paddle attachment, cream together the butter, sugar, and vanilla extract on medium speed, scraping down the bowl with a rubber spatula as needed, until smooth in color and light in texture, about 2 minutes. Blend in the egg yolk, scraping down the bowl as needed, until blended.

2. Add the flour all at once, mixing on low speed or by hand with a wooden spoon until just blended, about 30 seconds. (The dough will be very crumbly when you remove it from the mixer.) Wrap the dough tightly in plastic wrap and refrigerate for a minimum of 30 minutes before rolling out.

Zwiebach

KIDS AND adults alike will love these cookies; they are great for just munching or for dipping in a tall cool glass of milk. Even though these cookes are twice baked, the eggs keep them from becoming too hard.

2½ cups bread flour

1 tsp baking powder

¼ cup almond paste

1½ cups sugar

8 large eggs

2 tsp vanilla extract

1. Line sheet pans with parchment paper.

2. Sift together the bread flour and baking powder into a large mixing bowl.

3. Mix together the almond paste with ½ cup of the sugar in a mixing bowl. Add the eggs and the remaining cup of sugar, alternating in three additions and mixing to blend between each until incorporated and smooth. Place the bowl of the mixer over a hot water bath and whisk constantly until the mixture reaches 110°F.

4. Remove the mixture from the heat, add the vanilla extract and beat the mixture on medium speed, until cool, about 5 minutes. Gently fold in the sifted dry ingredients until just incorporated.

5. Fill a pastry bag fitted with a No.9 piping tip and pipe 12-in-long strips 1½ in wide.

6. Bake the zwiebach in a preheated 325°F until they just begin to brown, about 15 minutes. Remove from the oven and cut into strips ½ in wide. Arrange the zwieback cut side down on the pan and bake in a 275°F oven until dry.

STORAGE: The cookies can be stored in an airtight container for 3 weeks.

INDEX